E-Z Review™

for

Copyright Law

By

Allison B. Hoch, *Esq.*
Cardozo School of Law

Contributing Editors:

Amy B. Gitlitz, *Esq*.
Cardozo School of Law

Randy J. Riley, *Esq.*
Seton Hall Law School

Law Review Publishing
River Vale, NJ
(800) 371-1271

E-Z Review for Copyright Law

Editorial Staff

Printed in Canada

184 Central Avenue
Old Tappan, NJ 07675 - 2234
(800) 371-1271

Library of Congress

ISBN 1-887426-76-0

Note: This review publication is not meant to replace required texts as a substitute or otherwise. This publication should not be quoted from or cited to. It is meant only to be used as a reminder of some subject matter and is not a substitute for a comprehensive understanding of the actual materials which it references or outlines.

TABLE OF CONTENTS

I. Concept of Copyright Law

A. The Purpose of Copyright Law

Originally in the eighteenth century, the first English copyright act, the Statute of Anne of 1710, gave authors the exclusive right to make copies of their books.

In its broadest sense, copyright law creates a system of property rights for certain kinds of intangible products, generally known as works of authorship.

The term copyright is a highly descriptive term and refers to the right to make copies. It reflects the basic Anglo-American notion that undesirable economic results will occur if unimpeded copying is allowed of those intangible products whose production we wish to encourage.

The focus of copyright law is on the benefits derived by the public from the labors of authors. Under this view, reward to the copyright owner or author is a secondary concern.
Today's copyright law goes much farther in protecting works against copying in the strict sense of the word. Much of what we protect in copyright law today, such as performance rights, display rights, and derivative work rights, are more analogous to rights to use a work rather than to copy it. In addition, current copyright law covers much broader grounds, including not only most artistic, literary, and musical works, but computer software, databases, and architectural works.

B. The Concept of "Authorship"

The difference in terminology between the common law copyright and the civil law author's rights stems from a fundamental difference in attitude between the two legal traditions about works of authorship.

1. Common Law

The common law meaning for "copyright" is an impersonal one, removed from the author. It connotes a negative right in the owner to prevent copying of his work.
The general philosophy of copyright in the common law world is to provide material support to one who invests in producing the work, whether an individual author or corporate entity.

The ultimate goal of copyright is to enhance public welfare, an essentially economic value.

2. Civil Law

The civil law tradition views the author's work as an extension of his or her personality which springs into existence by a personal act of creation. This view reflects a more sympathetic attitude toward the author. Under the civil law system, an author is deemed to have a moral entitlement to control and exploit the product of his or her intellect. Under a principle of natural justice, the author, whose work is identified with his or her name throughout its existence, is given the right to publish his work as he or she sees fit, and to prevent its injury or mutilation.

C. Historical Development of Anglo-American Copyright Law

1. Early Developments

a. The Statute of Anne

The development of copyright law has been a continuing response to the challenge posed by new technologies that reproduce and distribute human expression. Indeed, the first copyright statute was a reaction to a new technology of the fifteenth century, the printing press.

In response to lobbying efforts, Parliament passed the first copyright act, the Statute of Anne, in 1710. The Statute of Anne rewarded authors for their creations, but at the same time recognized the public domain by limiting these rights to a specific number of years. For existing works, the Statute provided that "authors and their assigns" should have the sole right of publication (thereby seemingly breaking the stationers' historic monopoly) for 21 years. New books were given a first term of protection of 14 years for authors and their assigns, measured from the date of first publication, plus a second term of 14 years which reverted to the author if he lived to its commencement.

In *Donaldson v. Beckett*, the House of Lords established that the term of copyright is finite. Once that copyright term is exhausted, a work will fall into the "public domain."

The Statute of Anne defined a "copy" as being "the sale, liberty of printing, and reprinting of a book." Infringement occurred when a third party printed, reprinted, or imported the book without consent. The protection granted was basically no more than a prohibition against literal copying. To enforce his rights, an author had to register the title of the book with the Stationer's Company before publication.

On the whole, the Statute of Anne, which became the model for copyright law in the United States, articulated a series of mixed and contradictory messages about the purposes of copyright. On the one hand, copyright was viewed as an instrument in the service of the public interest. On the other hand, it could be considered the natural due of those who engage in artistic creation.

b. United States Constitution

The Framers of the Constitution recognized the need for a uniform federal law for copyright and patents. The result was Article I, § 8, cl. 8, which creates the Federal Government's right to legislate regarding copyright and patent: "Congress shall have power . . . . to promote the progress of science and useful Arts, by securing for limited Times, to Authors and Inventors, the exclusive Right to their respective Writings and Discoveries."

As revealed in the constitutional language (which does not even use the term "copyright"), the dominant idea is to promote the dissemination of knowledge to enhance public welfare. This goal is to be accomplished through an economic incentive in the form of a monopoly right given for limited times, and the beneficiary of this monopoly right is the author.

c. The Copyright Act of 1790

The first relevant legislation, Copyright Act of 1790, was passed pursuant to the new constitutional authority, and its provisions, modeled on the Statute of Anne, set the tone for future statutes, securing to authors and their assigns the rights to exploit maps, charts and books for two 14-year terms, an original term and a renewal term.

2. The 1909 Act

a. General Provisions of the 1909 Act

Under the 1909 Act, copyrightable subject matter was expanded to include "all the writings of an author." *See* 17 U.S.C. § 4 (1909 Act).
The 1909 Act included a bifurcated durational system a first term of 28 years from publication, plus a second 28-year renewal term, allowing copyright protection for a possible total of 56 years. *See* 17 U.S.C. § 24 (1909 Act).
Under the 1909 Act, federal copyright protection began the moment of publication (assuming affixation of a proper copyright notice), *see* 17 U.S.C. § 10 (1909 Act), not from the time the title of the work was filed for registration, as had previously been true.
Unpublished works were not covered by the 1909 Act, resulting in a dual system of state common law copyright for unpublished works and federal protection for published works.

b. The United States and the Berne Convention

One particular unfortunate feature of the 1909 Act was its failure to amend U.S. law to conform to the then relatively new Berne Convention for the Protection of Literary and Artistic Works.

The Berne Convention is the premiere treaty governing international copyright relations.

The Berne Convention made notice permissive instead of mandatory for copyright protection. However, registration was still a prerequisite for infringement suit for U.S. works but not foreign works. If you are registered, then that is *prima facia* evidence (no summary judgment allowed).

However, if you are not registered you automatically lose the right to collect attorney fees and statutory damages.
Two of the more prominent impediments were:

i. The 1909 Act's insistence on compliance with certain formalities as a prerequisite for copyright protection or work will fall into the public domain, *see* 17 U.S.C. § 10 (1909 Act), (Berne granted copyright protection absent compliance with formalities); and

ii. The 1909 Act's shorter term of copyright (Berne minimum requirement of the life of the author plus fifty years).

United States adherence to the Berne Convention has allowed that failing to place a copyright notice on the work is not automatically fatal to copyright protection. Although it does not automatically fail due to lack of copyright protection, it may still fail for other contributing reasons.

c. Legislative Attempts to Revise the 1909 Act

From 1909 until the passage of the 1976 Act, changing times and technologies forced Congress to amend the 1909 Act in major ways:

i. Motion pictures were added as a subject matter category (1912).
ii. Performance right for profit was provided for nondramatic literary works (1952).United States ratified the Universal Copyright Convention (U.C.C.) which provides nondiscriminatory protection to nationals of all member nations for works published within their borders (1954).
iii. No formalities are required for unpublished works.
iv. Published works must bear a prescribed copyright.

3. The Copyright Act of 1976

a. Important Changes Made by the 1976 Act

The 1976 Act made innovative changes in addition to clarifying certain aspects of existing law. The more important aspects of the Act include:

i. *Subject Matter*: The 1976 Act established broad categories of subject matter. *See* 17 U.S.C. § 102(a) (amended in 1990 to include architectural works as an eighth category).

ii. *The "exclusive rights" and their limitations*: § 106 of the 1976 Act enumerates five exclusive rights of copyright ownership. A new provision, § 106A, was added in 1990 to delineate rights in works of visual art. The sections immediately following § 106A impose various limitations on the exclusive rights. *See* 17 U.S.C. §§ 107-20.

iii. *Ownership*: Ownership of copyright is divisible under the 1976 Act, thus permitting the copyright owner to license or assign parts of the copyright "bundle of rights" to third parties, who can then exploit those rights themselves and bring suits for their infringement against others. *See* 17 U.S.C. § 201(d).

iv. *General preemption of common law copyright*: Every original work of authorship fixed in a tangible medium of expression is federally protected from the moment of creation. *See* 17 U.S.C. § 301.

v. *Duration*: For works created after it took effect, a basic single term of the life of the author plus 70 years. *See* 17 U.S.C. § 302(a). An alternate term of 95 years from publication or 120 years from creation, whichever is less, is provided for anonymous and pseudonymous works, and works made for hire. *See* 17 U.S.C. § 302(c).

vi. *Termination rights*: Inalienable option to terminate transfers of interest after specified periods of time. *See* 17 U.S.C. §§ 203, 304(c).

vii. *Formalities*: Initially, under the 1976 Act, notice was required for all published works, and it was possible to forfeit copyright by failure to affix notice. As of March 1, 1989, the use of copyright notice ceased to be mandatory. *See* 17 U.S.C. §§ 401(a) and 405. Registration of copyright and recordation of transfers of copyright were also a condition to bringing suits for infringement of these works until amendments, which took effect in 1989, eliminated the latter requirement and modified the former. *See* 17 U.S.C. § 411. These formalities have been modified by the Berne Convention Implementation Act of 1988. *See* 17 U.S.C. §§ 205, 411.

viii. *Fair use*: § 107 codifies the broadest exception to the § 106 exclusive rights: the judicially developed

ix. *Compulsory licenses*: The 1976 Act increased the number of compulsory licenses, which allow access to copyrighted works upon payment of the statutory fees and compliance with formalities. (Cable television (§ 111), mechanical recording (§ 115), jukebox (§ 116), public broadcasting (§ 118), and satellite home viewing (§ 119).)

x. *Entry into Berne*: It was not until the Berne Act amendments of 1988 that the impediments (formalities of notice and registration) to U.S. adherence were overcome.

* Invalidated the notice requirement. *See* 17 U.S.C. § 401

* Works published after March 1, 1989, notice is permissive and a copyright owner can no longer forfeit copyright by omitting notice of publicly distributed copies of the work. *See* 17 U.S.C. § 405.

* No longer need registration to bring an infringement suit against works originating from a Berne country.

* Recordation in the Copyright Office is no longer a prerequisite to bring an infringement suit. *See* 17 U.S.C. § 205(d).

b. Subsequent Developments Under the 1976 Act

In 1980, § 117 was completely amended providing protection for and establishing the scope of rights in computer programs.

Since 1978, the enactment of the Semiconductor Chip Protection Act of 1984 is a major development in copyright.

c. The Continuing Importance of the 1909 Act

Neither the 1976 Act nor any subsequent copyright legislation is retroactive. Thus, copyrighted works which entered the public domain under the 1909 Act are not revived by these Acts.

D. Justifications for Copyright Law

1. In General

These two approaches to copyright, one based on the natural rights of the author and the other on utilitarian principles (the economic rationale of copyright) which are the foundations of a system of copyright, are sometimes at cross purposes.

Arguments for establishing property rights are justified on two fundamental grounds:

a. Person's moral right to reap the fruits of his or her own labor (an idea based on natural law philosophy, including the ideology of authorship); and
b. Utilitarian rationale that views copyright law as an incentive system designed to produce an optimum quantity of works of authorship and thereby enhance the public welfare.

2. The Natural Law Justification

The natural law justification for recognizing property rights in works of authorship is based on the rights of authors to reap the fruits of their creations, to obtain rewards for their contributions to society, and to protect the integrity of their creations as extensions of their personalities.

John Locke's Theory: Copyright law, which confers an exclusive property right in an author's work, vindicates the natural right of individuals to control their works and be justly compensated for their contributions to society.

Criticism of the natural law justification:

i. How much control the author should have? How long that control should last? Who should benefit from the copyrighted work?

ii. The goal of fair compensation is at best a vague concept. No one can show what is the "fair" price for any commodity, service, or work of authorship.

3. The Incentive Rationale for Copyright Law

a. Generally

Rather than encouraging production of works by government subsidy, awards, or prizes, the author is given, through the limited monopoly of copyright law, a private property right in her creation, whose worth ultimately will be determined by the market. The underlying policy of this constitutional scheme is to promote the public welfare through private market incentives.

b. An Economic Argument for Rights in Intellectual Property

Intellectual property can be a great value, as well as costly to produce; without a legal regime protecting such products, the public welfare would suffer.
Free market economics disfavors the creation of monopolies unless there is an economic justification.

If an author cannot exclude others from her work, the result will be either non-production or non-disclosure. Viewed in this way, copyright law represents an economic trade-off between optimal creation of works of authorship and their optimal use.

* On the one hand, copyright provides the incentive to create new products and a shelter to develop and protect them.
* On the other hand, a copyright owner's monopoly right is limited in time and scope by such doctrines as originality, the idea/expression dichotomy, and fair use.

In the absence of copyright protection, self-help through market headstart is the traditional means by which an author or inventor can obtain a return on investment. But a head start advantage is only as good as the length of time it takes another to copy your product.

c. Copyright and "Interest Analysis"

Functionally, publishers, movie studios, record companies, and other entities which are not "authors" can best be understood as "distributors" or "disseminators" firms (or occasionally individuals) in the business of bridging the gap between individual creative workers and the ultimate consumers of their work.

4. The Future of Copyright

What seemed to be a farsighted, intelligently drafted statute is already obsolete in some ways. The reason is the time lag between technological and legal change.
Perceived threats posed by the new technology should not overshadow the fact that a copyright is a monopoly, whose basic term lasts the life of the author plus 50 years.

E. Related Bodies of Federal Law

Copyright law protects "original works of authorship."

Patent law provides a limited monopoly for new and inventive products, processes and designs.

Trademark law prohibits product imitators from passing off their goods or services as the products of others.

All three areas of intellectual property law recognize property rights in intangible products:

* copyright (expression)
* patent (technology)
* trademark (symbolic information).

These bodies of law, because they concern federally recognized rights, generally are governed by federal statutes and administered by federal agencies (except in the case of trademarks, as to which state law also may apply).

	COPYRIGHT	**PATENT**	**TRADEMARK**
Subject Matter	Literary, dramatic, and musical works; pantomimes and choreography; pictorial, graphic and sculptural works; audio-visual works; sound recordings; architectural works	Utility: Functional features of products and processes Design: Ornamental designs for manufactured goods	Words, names, symbols, or devices
Standards For Validity	Originality and fixation in a tangible medium of expression	Utility: Novelty, nonobviousness and utility Design: What is obvious to ordinary designer	Use of mark to distinguish one's goods or services
When Protection Begins	Upon fixation of original expression	Utility: Date of grant by U.S. Patent & Trademark Office (however, 20-year term measured from application date) Design: Date of grant by U.S. Patent & Trademark Office	Upon use of mark
Duration Of Protection	Life of the author (or longest-lived joint author), plus 70 years; or in the case of anonymous works, pseudonymous works, or works made for hire, 95 years from publication or 120 years from creation, whichever expires first	Utility: 20 years from application date (changed from 17 years from date issued) Design:14 years from date issued	So long as properly used as trademark
Standards For Infringement	Copying and improper appropriation	Utility: Making, using, selling or offering to sell the patented invention Design: Similarity of the designs to ordinary observer	Likelihood of confusion

F. State Intellectual Property Law

In addition to federal law, a diverse system of state intellectual property law also plays a significant role in protecting intangible property.

1. Trade Secret

Trade secret law protects much the same technological information as does patent law, but trade secret subject matter is even broader, extending to customer lists, marketing plans, and other information not included within patentable subject matter. In addition, a trade secret does not have to meet the rigorous standards of inventiveness required by patent law. A valid trade secret exists only if it is substantially "secret" within the trade secret's owner's industry; absolute secrecy is not required. Unlike a patent, a trade secret can potentially last forever.

2. Unfair Competition

Defined two ways:

a. A general area of law covering various commercial torts.

b. An action brought when one company passes off its goods or service as someone else's (narrower preferred sense).

3. Common Law Copyright

Common law copyright is almost entirely preempted by federal law. Although federal preemption casts a long shadow, state common law copyright might play a role when a work is not fixed in a tangible medium of expression. In practice, however, few courts have even considered copyright protection for oral works, but they have recognized its possibility.

4. The Right of Publicity

The right of publicity prohibits appropriation for commercial benefit of a celebrities' name, likeness, picture, or voice, for the celebrity has been deprived of a property right in the fruit of his labors (i.e., the ability to exploit commercially her name, likeness, picture, or voice). The right of publicity prohibits appropriation for commercial benefit of a person's name, likeness, picture or voice. The right of privacy relates to dignity harm, whereas the right to publicity involves commercial harm.

Whatever its form, the right of publicity is a more absolute right than either trademark or general unfair competition rights, and is based on a theory of unjust enrichment.

5. Misappropriation

Misappropriation doctrine is the broadest, and also the vaguest, theory protecting intangible property under state law. Causes for action for misappropriation have been successful where the traditional forms of intellectual property protection do not apply, but where a need for protection exists. Some courts have expressed a hostility toward the misappropriation doctrine, claiming that it conflicts with the policy underlying federal patent and copyright law and is therefore preempted under the Supremacy Clause of the Constitution.

ARTICLE I, § 8, CL. 8 OF THE U.S. CONSTITUTION:
"The Congress shall have Power . . . To Promote the Progress of Science and useful Arts, by securing for limited Times to Authors and Inventors the exclusive Right to their respective Writings and Discoveries."

The language of the Constitution is so open that it does not provide much guidance. It appears that the fewer words used, the broader the power it grants. This constitutional language was specialized for the era it was written:
"*Science*" refers to knowledge and wisdom.
"*useful Arts*" refers to crafts.
"*securing for limited Times . . . .*" means that one does not have a copyright forever.

The copyright clause is one of the enumerated clauses. Authors have the right over the distribution of the intellectual property aspect of work and should be able to sell their copyrights (similar to property rights).

* If the copyright is for a tangible item, then a limited number of people can enjoy it at the same time.
* If the copyright is for an intangible item, then an unlimited number of people can enjoy it at the same time without destroying creation.

One Needs To Balance Incentive To Author & Benefit To Society:

* Since there is a limited term, one needs to disseminate it as much as possible.

* Want society to eventually gain free access.
Need uniformity of the law to be able to enforce.
Federal system must preempt state (didn't do this until 1976 Act.).
Copyright law has lower standard (originality) than patent law (non obviousness).

Trademark law is covered under the Commerce Clause, not the copyright clause.

When Interpreting A Statute, One Should:

i. Look at language; and
ii. Look at legislative history (if can't get plain meaning from language of statute).

SOMETHING TO THINK ABOUT

Suppression Is Valuable Because:

i. Incentive system - award property rights to motivate others to create; if someone has labored with an idea, they should be compensated.
ii. Natural law theory - divine wisdom is protected.
iii. Reward system. Copyright only rewards the "original" expression of the idea (product), not the idea itself.

II. Subject Matter of Copyright Protection

Originality and fixation are two fundamental prerequisites for copyright protection under § 102(a).
§ 102(b), on the other hand, denies protection to works otherwise satisfying the Act's requirements if the copyright is claimed for any "*idea, procedure, process, system, method of operation, concept, principle, or discovery. . . .*"

A. Fixation

A work is incapable of protection under federal law unless it is "fixed" in a "tangible meaning of expression."

Only works which qualify as writings may claim federal copyright protection. The Supreme Court has construed the "writings" requirement to mean any physical rendering of the fruits of intellectual activity.

A copyright comes into existence when both a work of authorship and a material object merge through the act of fixation.

A work would be considered "fixed in a tangible medium of expression" if there has been an authorized embodiment in a copy or phono record and if that embodiment "is sufficiently permanent or stable" to permit the work "to be perceived, reproduced, or otherwise communicated for a period of more than transitory duration."

As a basic condition of copyright protection, the work must be fixed in a "tangible medium of expression," and this medium may be one "now known or later developed," and that the fixation is sufficient if the work "can be perceived, reproduced, or otherwise communicated, either directly or with the aid of a machine or device."

The concept of fixation is important not only because it determines whether the provisions of the statute apply to a work, but it also represents the dividing line between common law and statutory protection.

An unfixed work of authorship would continue to be subject to protection under State common law or statute, but would not be eligible for Federal statutory protection under § 102.

1. Perception by Machine or Device

The fixation requirement will be satisfied if the work as fixed can be perceived either directly or with the aid of a machine or device existing now or developed at a later time.

White-Smith Music Publishing Co. v. Apollo Co., 209 U.S. 1, 28 S. Ct. 319, 52 L. Ed 655 (1908)
The Supreme Court held that a piano roll was not a copy of the musical composition embodied on it and therefore did not qualify for copyright because there must be a printed record in intelligible notation, readable to the eye. (Doctrine applied to both phonorecords and magnetic tape, neither of which embody intelligible, eye-readable written notation.)
Thus, what is readable is copyrightable while what is audible is not. Language of statute does not cover perforated rolls of music. Perhaps the drafters never thought about this technology.

Today, under the Copyright Act, the White-Smith doctrine is completely ***overruled***, allowing copyrightability for sound recordings, computer programs, motion pictures, and other works embodied on objects which cannot be read without a machine or device.

SOMETHING TO THINK ABOUT:
The problem with trying to include future technology in © statute is that Congress can't keep up with technology. Therefore, the courts are deciding © law.
Majority in *White-Smith* was telling Congress that they made a mistake under strict language of the statute and Congress needs to expand its definition.
In reaction, Congress added the following language:

* § 102(a) → "now known or later developed"; also "either directly or with the aid of a machine or device."
* § 101 → See definition of "copies" and "fixed" (still room for interpretation).

Suppose you communicate on the internet with another person. None of your conversation is saved. You communicated by merely typing back and forth. Is this copyrightable?

NO - The communication was not permanent or stable and it was not communicated for a period of time that was longer than transitory.

Reasons For A Fixation Requirement:

i. It is a good way to establish intent (people who make effort to fix work).
ii. Fixed works are easily disseminated and the public gets something out of it in the future.

2. The Videogame Cases

The most recent analysis of the fixation requirement has involved actions for infringement of copyrighted video games, in which visual images and sounds are produced by computer programs stored in various memory devices. When the game is not being played, the images are repetitive. During play, however, they are subject to variation by human intervention. The defendants in several cases have claimed that they were free to copy the plaintiff's games because they were not fixed in a tangible medium of expression but were rather transitory projections on a cathode ray tube.

Midway Manufacturing Co. v. Arctic Int'l., Inc., 704 F.2d 1009 (7th Cir. 1982)
The court rejected the claim that the player's participation prevents the fixing of the audiovisual patterns, concluding that there is always a repetitive sequence of a substantial portion of the sights and sounds of the game. Many aspects of the display remain constant from game to game regardless of how the player operates the controls.

Thus, the fixation requirement does not require that the work be written down or recorded somewhere exactly as it is perceived by the eye. Rather, all that is necessary is that the work is capable of being perceived with the aid of a machine or device.

SOMETHING TO THINK ABOUT:

Can audiovisual aspect of the game be protected?
YES - It can be reproduced if one copies the exact human moves. Note that although the human eye can't read it all at any one moment, the machine can!

The Act now includes the language "either directly or with the aid of a machine or a device."

The Copyright Office used to allow filing by "literary works" and "audiovisual works." Now, proprietor must decide whether the "program" aspects or the "audiovisual" aspects predominate.

Courts are not happy to extend protection to things that are short lived, such as an ice sculpture or a poem in sand.
Suppose an author reads poetry to a crowd in a public park and someone else records it. Does the author have claim against the person who recorded it?
NO - The author must fix it to get protection. (§ 101 - "A work is 'fixed' . . . "by or under the authority of the author").
Protection arises simultaneously with fixation. (If author and other both tape, author protect against other immediately.)

B. Originality

There are two aspects of originality as developed by the courts and now embodied in § 102(a):

i. Independent creation by the author; and
ii. A modest quantum of creativity.

Copyright protects an author's expression of her idea, but not the idea itself.

"Original, as the term is used in copyright, means only that the work was independently created by the author (opposed to copied from other works), and that it possesses at least some minimal degree *(de minimis*) of creativity. *(See Feist Publications, Inc. v. Rural Telephone Service Co., Inc.)*
It should be noted that *Feist* is about the law of authorship and that the court's definition of "originality" applies equally to claims of copyright protection for works of all descriptions.

Originality requires independent creation plus a modicum of creativity. Reproductions are also copyrightable.

In copyright law, all that is required for protection is independent creation, not striking uniqueness, ingenuity, or novelty.

SOMETHING TO THINK ABOUT:
Suppose some art students go to the Metropolitan Museum of Art and copy a painting. The art school collects students efforts and publishes students work in book. The art school made $150,000

from the book. Can the students sue the art school for copyright infringement?

Maybe:

* The idea of the painting is not protected, but the expression (interpretation of the painting) is protected.
* Fact dependent (perhaps something in tuition contract that gives school all the rights to work created while in school).
* This is a hard case because it depends on who painted it.

Must Show Sufficient Originality.
There is no definition of originality in the statute. The drafters wanted to keep an evolution of meaning and not change it.
The phrase "original works of authorship," which is purposely left undefined, is intended to incorporate without change the standard of originality established by the courts under the present copyright statute. This standard does not include requirements of novelty, ingenuity, or aesthetic merit, and there is no intention to enlarge the standard of copyright protection to require them.

Copyright does not preclude others from using the ideas or information revealed by the author's work.

§ 102(b) makes clear that copyright protection does not extend to any idea, procedure, process, system, method of operation, concept, principle, or discovery, regardless of the form in which it is described, explained, illustrated, or embodied in such work.

Alfred Bell & Co. v. Catalda Fine Arts, Inc., 191 F.2d 99 (2d Cir. 1951) (Mezzotint engravings of old masters.)
In general, an artistic reproduction which merely makes an exact copy of a prior work would lack sufficient originality. If the copy, however, entails the independent creative judgment of the artist in its production, those aspects will render the work original.
A modest grade of originality is all that is required for copyrightability.

SOMETHING TO THINK ABOUT:
Is product copyrightable? Is the engravings sufficiently original or just a mere copy (The same as a photocopy or not)?
YES - It is sufficiently original. Copyright law rewards work and effort (and give property right). No two engravers can produce

identical interpretation of the same oil painting. Masters paintings fall into public domain.

Why Is One Willing To Grant © Protection?

i. To promote the arts and science and as an incentive.
ii. Adds to share of cultural treasures.
iii. Don't protect copies, but protect different expressions of the same idea.

Can't look at copyright as a method of awarding effort. There is State law protection for this.
Copyright law only rewards the PRODUCT, not the producer. *Intent* plays almost no role in copyright law. Thus, an unintentional variation may be rewarded a copyright because the public wants the product whether or not it was creative.

Originality Requires:

i. Independent Creation;
ii. Creativity - distinguishable variation.

Originality looks to see if it is distinguishable.
Process of engraving is not protected.

Atari Games Corp. v. Oman, 888 F.2d 878 (D.C. Cir. 1989) (Breakout - bricks (various colors), ball, and paddle)
In determining whether a work meets the quantum of originality, the work must be evaluated as a whole, not dissected as to its individual components.

Copyright Office improperly denied registration to a videogame screen. Copyright office focused on the independent components of the screens made up of simple geometric shapes.

The Office should have evaluated the work as a whole because even simple geometric shapes, when selected and combined in a distinctive manner, may meet the modest standard for creative authorship.
Originality can be bringing together of mundane objects (series of audio-visual protected). One needs to look at the totality of the work.

SOMETHING TO THINK ABOUT:
You take a photograph of your son in your yard. After you finish the roll, you bring it in to a store to have it developed. Suppose you see

the picture of your son from your film hanging in the store. Do you have a copyright in the picture?
Yes - The picture is fixed and original.

Is product sufficiently original?
Yes. No one looks like your son in your yard. The pose chosen is attractive and worthy of preservation. If the picture is original, then it is copyrightable. Therefore, all family photo's are copyrightable.

Burrow-Giles Lithographic Co. v. Sarony, 111 U.S. 53, 4 S. Ct. 279, 28 L. Ed. 349 (1884) (Photograph of Oscar Wilde)
Oscar Wilde was subject of photograph. Photographer dressed and positioned his pose.

One gets protection for mechanical reproductions because a photograph is a natural moment captured. Thus, separate from the mechanical part there is a separate copyright for the express vision, graphic, and artistic elements.

SOMETHING TO THINK ABOUT:

Suppose a second photographer creates the same picture. Is this Copyright infringement?
NO - Even if in the same clothes, there was not the same positioning, lighting, furniture, hand movement, etc.

Therefore, courts awarding creativity and originality by making qualitative assessment of end product.

What is protected with a mechanical reproduction?
Not merely pushing of the button, but rather the author's view. This is different than *Alfred Bell & Co. v. Catalda Fine Arts, Inc.*

Suppose a computer writes a short story. Is there © protection in it?
YES - It is fixed.

To determine originality:

i. Look at universe of possible works and existing works.
ii. Source in an author and sufficient creativity (distinguishable variation).

Why protect a short story?
Incentive - write more stories.
Lockean Property Theory - labor to create machine, property rights.
Reward - Look to product and reward product with property rights.

All we care is that product is sufficiently original to grant copyright.

Note: There is a policy against giving computer copyright protection.

Bleistein v. Donaldson Lithographing Co., 188 U.S. 239, 23 S. Ct. 298, 47 L.Ed. 460 (1903) (Copyrightability of Wallace's circus ad)
Although the requirement of creative authorship entails a certain de minimis amount of originality, it embodies no conception of artistic merit or beauty. Thus, the court should not sit and judge what is art. Since Bleistein, both courts and the Copyright Office have avoided aesthetic decisions in deciding questions of originality.
This case involved the question of whether a copyright could be claimed for a work intended for advertising purposes. The earlier view was that copyright protection was denied for advertisements. However, some non-artistic works, such as maps or ledgers, were protected. Today, however, so long as the work contains the required original elements, courts will not look to the intended purpose of the work or the audience to whom it is directed.

"Others are free to copy the original. They are not free to copy the copy." Judges evaluate work compared to universe of possible works (in essence, they judge art). Thus, originality requires some evaluation by the court. Just because something is an advertisement and public cannot see the value now, courts are afraid to deny protection because it might be valuable later.

1. The Idea/Expression Dichotomy

Section 102(b) of the Copyright Act codifies the principle that copyright protects the expression of an idea but not the idea itself by denying copyright protection to any idea, procedure, process, system, method of operation, concept, principle, or discovery, regardless of the form in which it is described, explained, illustrated, or embodied in such work.

Once an author reveals his work to the public, he injects the idea into the public domain and must be content to maintain control only over the form in which the idea is expressed.

To create new works, future authors must have access to a well-endowed pubic domain, the place where fundamental building materials concepts, discoveries, and technological solutions reside and are freely available for those wishing to embellish them with their own original expression.

As in the case of originality, the idea-expression distinction is left undefined in the Copyright Act.
Separating an idea from its expression is an ad hoc process, and how broadly a court defines what constitutes the idea as compared to the expression depends on the nature of the subject matter at issue.

* If the idea is defined too broadly, it will create a bottleneck impeding production of future works.
* On the other hand, if the idea is defined too narrowly, future authors will not have sufficient economic incentive to create new work.

Baker v. Selden, 101 U.S. 99, 11 S. Ct. 99, 25 L. Ed. 841 (1880) (Selden published Selden's Condensed Ledger of Bookkeeping Simplified with forms and explanations of use.)
Because functional works often closely integrate idea and expression, they tend to conflict with copyright law's protection of original expression. Interests of utility will frequently compel expression in functional works "to hew closely to the underlying and unprotectable idea, procedure, process, system or method of operation that it express."

When encountering a functional work, the courts will limit protection to avoid conferring a de facto monopoly over the unprotectable, utilitarian aspects of the work. Distinguishing between idea and expression is a difficult but necessary task because of the policies that differentiate copyright from patent law.

The Supreme Court reversed a judgment for the plaintiff, reasoning that the system could not be used absent the methods and diagrams in the book. Thus, according to the Court, the ledger was actually a utilitarian object rather than an expressive work. Unless copyright were denied in this instance, a monopoly could in effect be granted over the underlying idea of the system.

We should not allow a creator of inherently patentable subject matter, i.e., a system or process, to use copyright law to circumvent the patent system.

Where the use of an idea requires the copying of the work itself, such copying will not constitute infringement. On the other hand, if the copying does not involve the use of the art but instead its explanation, then such copying will constitute an infringement.

2. Merger Doctrine

There are some instances where the use of a system or process necessitates the identical copying of the author's expression of the system or process. In other words, if the underlying idea (or system, process, or method of operation) can effectively be expressed in only one way, the idea and expression are said to have "merged." When this occurs, the work cannot receive protection under copyright law. To allow copyright protection in such an instance would undermine the distinction between copyright and patent law.

SOMETHING TO THINK ABOUT:
Why don't we want copyright protection for system?

i. System is knowledge and we do not want to stop knowledge.
ii. Without form a system is useless.
iii. Want to foster competition.
iv. Want to encourage advancement.

Never grant copyright for system but a more complex form can get protection.

If form sufficiently original, will be granted protection (resembles patent protection).

Is there © protection for "I am going to the store?"
NO - Not protected because language gets you through everyday business and everyone else need this language.

Kern River Gas Transmission Co. v. Coastal Corp., 899 F.2d 1458 (5th Cir. 1990) (Map created and given out in public domain.)
The plaintiff's depiction of its proposed natural gas pipeline route on government survey maps was not copyrightable. The maps may have been original, but, according to the court, they expressed the idea of the location of the pipeline in the only effective way. Thus, when idea and expression are inseparable they merge, precluding copyright protection.

There is only one way in which the map can be drawn. Thus, if grant copyright protection, suppress expression as well as idea. Under Merger Doctrine, expression of certain ideas are not copyrightable because there exists only a very limited number of ways of expressing each idea. (Certain core ways of expression linked to idea.)

SOMETHING TO THINK ABOUT:
Suppose two people create identical individual works at same time. Who gets the copyright?
Neither - Cannot win on this claim because inconsistent with originality. One had access to other's work (subconscience). Also, the two works are too close (identical) that court must assume one copied from the other.

C. Works of Authorship

One should always make the distinction between the copyright on the work of authorship and the object in which the work is fixed.

The list of categories of works of authorship in § 102(a) of the 1976 Act is meant to be illustrative, rather than limitative. The categories are not only broad, but also overlapping.
Of the eight categories listed, four are defined in § 101. Three of the undefined categories "musical works," "dramatic works," and "pantomimes and choreographic works" have fairly settled meanings.

The four items defined in § 101 are;

i. Literary works;
ii. Pictorial, graphic, and sculptural works;
iii. Motion pictures and audiovisual works; and
iv. Sound recordings.

In each of these cases, definitions are needed not only because the meaning of the term itself is unsettled but also because the distinction between "work" and "material object" requires clarification.
The definition of "pictorial, graphic, and sculptural works" carries with it no implied criterion of artistic taste, aesthetic value, or intrinsic quality.

In the Supreme Court's decision *Mazer v. Stein*, works of "applied art" encompass all original pictorial, graphic, and sculptural works that are intended to be or have been embodied in useful articles, regardless of factors such as mass production, commercial exploitation, and the potential availability of design patent protection.

The declaration that "pictorial, graphic, and sculptural works" include "works of artistic craftsmanship insofar as their form but not their mechanical or utilitarian aspects are concerned" is classic language.

A "useful article" is defined as "an article having an intrinsic utilitarian function that is not merely to portray the appearance of the article or to convey information."

The test of separability and independence from "the utilitarian aspects of the article" does not depend upon the nature of the design that is, even if the appearance of an article is determined by aesthetic (as opposed to functional) consideration, only elements , if any which can be identified separately from the useful article as such are copyrightable.

Copyrightable "sound recordings" are original works of authorship comprising and aggregate of musical, spoken, or other sounds that have been fixed in tangible form. The copyrightable work comprises the aggregation of sounds and not the tangible medium of fixation.

Deciding whether a writing will be considered a work of authorship is a two-step process:

i. One must determine whether the legislative history has expressly excluded it. Examples of express exclusion are industrial design and typeface design, which Congress has explicitly indicated are not to be considered works of authorship.
ii. Even absent express exclusion, one must determine whether the writing has been historically excluded. This determination requires a return to the case law under the 1909 Act. An example of writings which have been historically excluded and which have not been expressly included by the Copyright Act or the legislative history are literary characters and title.

Ultimately, a court would decide whether a work fits into one category or another. However, the Copyright Office has an influential role in determining into which category a work falls.

Explanations of Levels:

i. House/Senate statement made on floor following enactment; President statement during signing (has spin on it, not very reliable).
ii. Failure of action = (legislature approve of action) or (that they didn't get act together to meet).

iii. Public statements to press; not there to serve best interest of entire country; *Special interest written to persuade. (All copyright legislation written by nonlegislative drafters)*
iv. Congress operates as a rubber stamp, they will not modify or amend.
v. For © legislation, we have no legislative drafters.
vi. Debate about meeting or purpose, not in writing, no connection to writing of Act.
vii. Will know what proposal doesn't mean, rejection usually.
viii. Outside interest brought legislation and why.
ix. Especially Joint Reports.

SOMETHING TO THINK ABOUT:
Suppose there exists a poster composed of computer chips that cause the image to constantly change. Can it be granted copyright protection?
Is this work covered by act? Look to § 102.
Maybe under §102(a)(5) - "pictorial, graphic, and sculptural works," when look to § 101, maybe not within language.
But language of § 102: "Works of authorship include the following categories:" this language is not limiting.
Maybe argue motion picture (similar to this), or somewhere in between picture and motion picture.

D. The Categories of Original Works

Notice also that the § 102(a) list, as indicated by the definition of "including" in § 101, is "illustrative and not limitative," so as to allow the courts as much flexibility as possible to adapt the law to new technologies and media. Furthermore, each enumerated category is liberal defined.

Congress in 1976 purposely chose the phrase "original works of authorship" to describe what it wanted to protect, after the courts had found it necessary to limit judicially the seemingly more expansive language of the 1909 Act, "all the writings of an author."

It is consistent in separating works of authorship from the material objects, (i.e., the copies or phonorecords) in which they might be embodied. But regardless of the media in which they are embodied, the novel remains a literary work and the ballad remains a musical work.

1. Literary Works

Literary works are defined by the 1976 Act as "works, other than audiovisual works, expressed in words, numbers, or other verbal or numerical symbols or indicia, regardless of the nature of the material objects, such as books, periodicals, manuscripts, phonorecords, film, tapes, disks, or cards, in which they are embodied."

This category encompasses all works written in words or symbols of any kind, regardless of the material objects in which they are embodied. The word "literary," in this context, implies no idea of literary merit. A literary work can be a computer program, a catalog, a data base, or a poem, written on a piece of paper or recorded on cassette. Copyright in computer programs is one form of literary work which has caused much controversy in recent years.

Miller v. Universal City Studios, Inc., 650 F.2d 1365 (5th Cir. 1981)
Plaintiff spent 2,500 hours in the preparation of a book involving a notorious Georgia kidnapping in which the victim was imprisoned in an underground coffin.
Despite some pronouncements in the case law that historical research in itself can be the basis of copyright, the recent trend in the case law, even before *Feist*, was to refuse copyright protection based on the industrious effort of the researcher.

The kidnapping victim and the reporter collaborated on the book. Universal Studios, after unsuccessful attempts to secure movie rights, nevertheless made a movie based entirely on the book.

The District Court declared itself in favor of the copyrightability of research. Its justification was based on a rationale similar to the telephone directory compilation cases: to reward the effort and ingenuity involved in giving expression to facts and to the effort required to unearth the facts.

The Court of Appeals for the Fifth Circuit reversed the District Court decision because it was unable to identify any appropriation of original expression. The court distinguished the telephone directory cases as constituting a category in themselves rather than extending their questionable logic to another setting.

According to the Fifth Circuit, copyright should be based only on the resulting writing and the original elements of authorship expressed in the work. The court could find "no rational basis for distinguishing between facts and the research involved in obtaining facts."

If the historian holds out the events as factual matter, they enter into the public domain, despite the strangeness or the improbability of their occurrence.

If one is allowed to copyright research, then everyone is going to have to start from ground zero (not efficient). Protection is not granted because the courts would rather only one person do the research and have other expand and build on existing work.

Apple Computer, Inc. v. Franklin Computer Corp., 714 F.2d 1240 (3d Cir. 1983) (Defendant Franklin copied Apple's O/S program to manufacture an Apple compatible computer.)

The court was confronted with three basic issues about the scope of protection for computer programs:

i. Whether copyright can exist in a computer program expressed in object code;
ii. Whether copyright can exist in a computer program embedded in a ROM; and
iii. Whether copyright can exist in an O/S program.

The court answered all three issues affirmatively, both reaffirming and expanding the scope of protection for computer programs.

i. The court had little trouble in concluding that a work written in object code unintelligible to humans would qualify as a literary work. Section 102(a) states that copyright protection extends to works fixed in any tangible means of expression "from which they can be perceived . . . with the aid of a machine or device," and does not require that they be intelligible to humans.
ii. The court had no difficulty repeating that the statutory requirement of fixation was satisfied because the ROM computer chip constituted the

material object in which the copyrighted work, i.e., the program, was embedded.

iii. Franklin claimed that the O/S was per se uncopyrightable under *Baker v. Selden* (merger doctrine). This argument states the doctrine of "merger" in which a work is uncopyrightable if its idea and expression merge, or are so closely related that one cannot be used without the other. Here, the Third Circuit found that the trial court had made insufficient findings as to whether idea and expression had merged, and remanded the case on this issue.

The court, however, unequivocally upheld the copyrightability of computer programs, whether application or O/Ss.
Franklin has established the copyrightability of O/S programs and the illegality of copying the programmer's expression manifested in the program.

The court did not define the difference between idea and expression as applied to computer programs. In the computer program context, one can equate idea with the accomplishment of a given task or function. Thus, if there are other ways to achieve the same result, there are alternative means of expression, and the doctrine of merger does not apply. Copyright should not be used to monopolize a result: the very essence of § 102(b).

The *Franklin* court, however, fell short of establishing 100% compatibility as the uncopyrightable "idea." In addition, it did not indicate either what degree of compatibility or how this compatibility could be achieved.

SOMETHING TO THINK ABOUT:
To see if "Computer Something" is covered under copyright, look at:
§ 102: It may be considered a "literary work" under
§ 102(a)(1) or "pictorial, graphic, and sculptural works" under
§ 102(a)(5).
§ 101: "Literary works" - expressed in words, numbers
Object code - in binary (0 & 1).
Source code - human write & converted to object code by compiler.

Don't care if humans can read object code because it can be ready by use of machine (*White-Smith* Doctrine overruled).
Courts have rejected the idea of protecting a process (patentable issue).

Computer programs not explicitly excluded from protection and no legislative history (Congress gives no guidance) to advise: Courts writing statute as they go along.

2. Computer Software Protection
In the United States, original works become protected under copyright laws when it is "fixed in a tangible medium." In most circumstances an original piece of software becomes "fixed" when the data is stored on a hard or floppy disk. However, the problem of registering is another issue that is later discussed.

The group of cases of which *Apple v. Franklin* is the most important sometimes is referred to as the "first generation" of software protection decision. Once that choice had been made in favor of protection, there arose a whole set of additional dilemmas, often referred to as "second generation" software protection issues: the fact that a work is protected by copyright does not mean that every element of that work is protected, not that every protected element is protected completely.

There are many ways to infringe the copyright in a conventional "literary work" without copying it word-for-word in its entirety.

Traditionally, where conventional works are concerned, experts have been barred from contributing to this inquiry into so-called "substantial similarity." But the *Whelan* court *(see e.g. Whelan Assoc. Int'l. v. Jaslow Dental Laboratory, Inc., 797 F. 2d 1222 (3d Cir. 1983))* stated that it would join "the growing number of courts which do not apply the ordinary observer test in copyright cases involving exceptionally difficult materials, like computer programs.

Ultimately, the *Whelan* court's conclusion that "copyright protection of computer programs may extend beyond the programs' literal code to their structure, sequence, and organization" is based, in principal part, on an analogy drawn between programs and other, more traditional copyrightable works.

In ***Computer Associates International, Inc. v. Altai, Inc.***, 982 F.2d 963 (2d Cir. 1992) the court approves a three-step procedure (Abstraction-Filtration-Comparison) for evaluating claims of substantial similarity in such cases:

i. The plaintiff's work is first put through processes of "abstraction" and "filtration," designed to "sift out all elements of the allegedly infringed program which are 'ideas' or are dictated by efficiency or external factors, or taken from the public domain;"
ii. Then, and only if "there [remains] a core of copyrighted material," this "golden nugget" is put through the final process;
iii. Finally, make a "Comparison" with the allegedly infringing work.

The implications of the *Computer Associates* approach for copyright protection of computer screen display formats remain uncertain. One line of cases treat the screen display which function as "user interfaces" as separate works, whether or not subject to separate copyright registration, and in particular as "compilations" of terms and symbols. In the decisions which forms the other groups, screen display formats are treated as protected aspects of the computer program work. Either way, we must deal with the argument that the software developer's unprotected "idea" is merged with its expression where screen display formats are concerned, and the related argument that, in any event, a "user interface" display is a "useful article" and therefore not subject to copyright protection where its utilitarian (as distinct from merely decorative) features are concerned.

The order in which commands are listed in a menu has a very limited functional value and is protectable.

The "reverse engineering" issue is this: to what extent should software developers be permitted, as a matter of copyright doctrine, to manipulate their competitors' products so as to discover the basic, unprotectable programming ideas on which those products are based? Two important Court of Appeals decisions have indicated that a solution to the "reverse engineering" problem may lie in the doctrine of "fair use."

3. Musical Works

The legislative history to the 1976 Copyright Act states that the term "musical works"(treated in § 102(a)(2)) is left undefined because they have "fairly settled meaning."

Musical works include both the instrumental component of the work and any accompanying words. Taking either the lyrics or the music alone infringes a musical work. Where musical works are concerned, one of the most valuable exclusive rights of the copyright owner is the right to prepare and distribute what used to be called "musical reproductions" - a category which, over time, has included recordings in forms ranging from piano rolls to "digital audio tapes." The 1976 Act refers to these as "phonorecords" and recognizes the rights of the musical work copyright owner in § 106.

The Copyright Act was amended in 1971 to create a new category of protected works, "sound recordings," which arise out of the joint "authorship" of those who participate in the phonogram production process generally as employees of production companies which acquire the resultant copyrights by virtue of assignment or by operation of the "work for hire" doctrine.

4. Dramatic Works

The legislative history to the 1976 Copyright Act states that the term "dramatic works"(§ 102(a)(3)) is left undefined because they have "fairly settled meaning".

Dramatic works category illustrates how various categories in the § 102(a) list may overlap one another.

Music accompanying a dramatic work could be copyrighted separately rather than under the dramatic works category.

The script for a dramatic work could be protected as a literary work.

A film dramatization of a screenplay is protected as a motion picture. Since the list of § 102(a) is illustrative and not limitative, it serves the minimal purpose of making it clear that plays, screenplays and other dramatizations of works are protectable.

5. Pantomimes and Choreographic Works

The legislative history to the 1976 Copyright Act states that the terms "pantomimes and choreographic works" (§ 102(a)(4)) are left undefined because they have "fairly settled meaning."

Pantomimes and Choreographic Works were added to the statutory catalogue of copyrightable works for the first time in the 1976 Act. These works may be protected if the necessary prerequisites are met:

i. The work must be fixed in a tangible medium; and
ii. The work must contain original routines or original arrangements of preexisting routines.

6. Pictorial, Graphic, and Sculptural Works

"Pictorial, graphic, and sculptural works" is listed in §102(a)(5) and defined in § 101 by means of an illustrative list, which includes "two-dimensional and three-dimensional works of find, graphic, and applied art, photographs, prints and art reproductions, maps, globes, charts, technical drawings, diagrams, and models."

The term "pictorial, graphic, and sculptural works" encompasses works of fine as well as applied art and implied no criteria of aesthetic value or taste. The aspect of this category which has engendered the most controversy is the role of copyright in protecting artistic creations embodying utilitarian objects.

The principal issue, not surprisingly, has been originality rather than fixation.

To meet the standard of originality, the creator of a map must engage in at least a modicum of direct observation. Case law under the 1976 Act has tended to reject the "sweat of the brow" requirement for copyrightability in maps, treating the standard the same as for other factual compilations.

SOMETHING TO THINK ABOUT
Suppose you design a lava lamp with. a lamp shade on top. Does it get protection?
No - It doesn't get protection for the lava lamp or the lamp shade. Separate out usefulness from art (creative aspect) and see what would get protected.

Is there copyright protection for a lava lamp without lava and fish inside?
No - Lava lamp is not granted protection for shape of glass, utilitarian changing sculpture, or natural phenomenon.
See § 101 for definition of "pictorial, graphic, and sculptural works." Protection granted if design incorporated pictorial, graphic or sculptural features that can be identified separately from, and are capable of existing independently.
The goal of the law has been to grant protection to the aesthetic features of an object without unduly extending the monopoly to its functional or mechanical features. It is often impossible, however, to separate in a rational way the aesthetic aspect of the article from its utilitarian dimension.

Mazer v. Stein**,** 347 U.S. 201, 74 S. Ct. 460, 98 L. Ed 630 (1954) (Copyrightability of statuettes of Balinese dancers used for bases of lamps.)
Copyright protection was limited to works of artistic craftsmanship insofar as their form, but not as to their mechanical or utilitarian aspects, as in jewelry, enamels, glassware, and tapestries.

The Supreme Court upheld the Copyright Office's regulation allowing copyright for works embodied in useful objects as to their form, but not as to their mechanical or utilitarian features. In addition, the Court also held that protection by design patent did not bar copyright protection.

After *Mazer v. Stein*, the use to which a work of art was put became irrelevant, but the question remained whether the whole range of industrial design in useful articles could qualify for copyright. In addition to these mass-produced objects, graphic designs for textiles were also included within copyrightable subject matter. While the statuettes' were copyrightable, we do not allow copyrightability of an automobile, a toaster, or a modernistic lighting fixture because their artistic aspects are of an abstract nature often fused with the functional attributes of the object. Unless the shape of an automobile, airplane, lady's dress, food processor, television set, or any other industrial product contains some element that, physically or conceptually, can be identified as separable from the utilitarian aspects of the article, the design would not be copyrighted under the bill. A work is creative if aesthetic element is primary and utilitarian element is secondary.

SOMETHING TO THINK ABOUT
What if Mazer v. Stein was decided in 1981?

It would have come out the same under the separability distinction - Protecting statuette, not lamp (separate) in 1954 (physical separation).
Look at statute (Copyright Act of 1976) § 102, then
§ 101 - "Pictorial, graphic, and sculptural works"
Kieselstein-Cord (belt buckle; applied the conceptual-separability test) decided in 1980 but Copyright Act of 1976 not applied because case started before the 1976 Act was enacted.
Carol Barnhart Inc. v. Economy Cover Corp., 773 F.2d 411 (2d Cir. 1985) (Plaintiff produced human torsos used to display articles of clothing).
The court found that the claimed artistic features, the life-size breast form and the width of the shoulders, were inextricably related to their utilitarian function, i.e., the display of clothes. The majority granted summary judgment for the defendant because the torsos utilitarian articles are not separate works of art. Therefore, not copyrightable.
The dissent was troubled with result and by its absence of a unifying test for conceptual separability. It proposed a test: for design features to be conceptually separate from the utilitarian aspects of the useful article that embodies the design, the article must stimulate in the mind of the beholder a concept that is entirely separable from the utilitarian functions.

SOMETHING TO THINK ABOUT:

Is a bar of soap sculpture copyrightable?
Conceptual separability. A sculpture made out of soap is copyrightable, but the soap is not.
Why don't you want to protect picture of torsos but will protect work of well-known artist?
Artist - protect expression of idea.
If someone spills paint on carpet, it won't be protected because there was no idea (mistake).

Only protect expression.
Someone can do something unintentionally and after can see result and say expression of idea.

Interpretation is everything in copyright law.
Mere declaration is not enough for originality; if photographer feels "SUN in rug" art, then now becomes copyrightable.

What do we do with originality requirement to help alleviate fear that Judge will apply personal feeling?
Set standard to be very low.
Need To Ask: Whether have distinguishable variation (not whether aesthetic).
If object is ©, © from moment it is fixed. However, couldn't identify © until later in time. © works evolve (never full intention to be ©).
Language of statute not clear about separability;
Two views:

i. Physical separation; and
ii. Conceptual separation.
(Courts confused about what view to follow.)

7. Motion Pictures and Other Audiovisual Works

§ 102(a)(6) of the 1976 Act specifically includes among the subject matter of copyright the category described as "motion pictures and other audiovisual works." Notice, however, that in § 102(a)(6), motion pictures are treated as a subcategory of audiovisual works.

The key language in the statutory definition ("series of related images") raises several issues:

i. Is it necessary that the images be presented serially sequentially, in a fixed, invariable order? NO.
ii. What is meant by the requirement that the image be related?
iii. What is the proper approach to be adopted in determining whether a work satisfies the quantum-of-originality requirement? Clearly, a work can qualify as an audiovisual work even though it consists of images which, individually, qualify for protection as pictorial, graphic or sculptural works.

Soundtracks of motion pictures are specifically included in the definition of "motion pictures," and excluded in the definition of "sound recordings." To be a "motion picture," as defined, requires three elements:

i. A series of images;

ii. The capability of showing the images in certain successive order; and
iii. An impression of motion when the images are thus shown.

It does not include:

i. Unauthorized fixation of live performances or telecasts;
ii. Live telecasts that are not fixed simultaneously with their transmission; or
iii. Filmstrips and slide sets which, although consisting of a series of images intended to be shown in succession, are not capable of conveying an impression of motion.

8. Sound Recordings

Sound recordings are defined in § 101 as "works that result from the fixation of a series of musical, spoken, or other sounds, but not including the sounds accompanying a motion picture or other audiovisual work, regardless of the nature of the material objects, such as discs, tapes, or other phonorecords, in which they are embodied." Sound recordings, however, archetypically involve musical works.

It is easy to confuse the sound recording with the musical work. The musical work is the "tune," plus any accompanying lyrics, as created by the composer. The sound recording is the "rendition" of the song as embodied in the phonorecord, including such components as the way the song is sung by the vocalist, played by the instrumentalists, arranged by the musical director, mixed by the recording engineer, and so on. The vocalist, instrumentalist, musical director and engineer, in other words, are the creators of the work, and their expression is the sound recording, not the song which is the composer's expression, and a separately copyrighted work. § 102(a)(7) protects the particular aggregate of sounds collected in the copyrighted work called the "sound recording," not the song being recorded (the "musical work") nor the physical object in which the sound recording and the musical work are embodied (the "phonorecord").

A sound recording must satisfy the ordinary prerequisites for a copyright: originality and fixation.

9. Architectural Works

The current U.S. Copyright Act expressly includes "diagram, models, and technical drawings, including architectural plans" as a species of protected "pictorial, graphic, and sculptural work."

The Committee concluded that the design of a work of architecture is a "writing" under the Constitution and fully deserves protection under the Copyright Act.

Under the "Architectural Works Copyright Protection Act of 1990," an "architectural work" is defined as "the design of a building as embodied in any tangible medium of expression, including a building, architectural plans, or drawings."

The work includes "the overall form as well as the arrangement and composition of spaces and elements in the design, but does not include individuals standard features."

* "Design" includes the overall form as well as the arrangement and composition of spaces and elements in the design.
* "Arrangement and composition of spaces and elements" recognizes that:
    i. Creativity in architecture frequently takes the form of a selection, coordination, or arrangement of unprotectable elements into an original, protectable whole;
    ii. An architect may incorporate new, protectable design elements into otherwise standard, unprotectable building features; and
    iii. Interior architecture may be protected.

The definition makes clear that protection does not extend to individual standard features.
Architectural work is deliberately not encompassed as pictorial, graphic, or sculptural works; therefore, the copyrightability of architectural works shall not be evaluated under the separability test applicable to pictorial, graphic, or sculptural works embodied in useful article.

Two step analysis is envisioned:

i. An architectural work should be examined to determine whether there are original design elements present, including overall shape and interior architecture;

ii. Examine whether the design elements are functionally required.

Determinations of infringement of architectural works are to be made according to the same standard applicable to all other forms of protected subject matter.

A new § 120 of Title 17, U.S.C., limiting the exclusive rights in architectural works, provides that state and local landmark, historic preservation, zoning, or building codes relating to architectural works protected under § 102(a)(8) are not preempted by the Copyright Act.

The bill is prospective, protecting:

i. "Architectural works created on or after the date of enactment"; These works will be governed by § 302 of title 17, United States Code: that is, works created by individuals will have a copyright measured by the life of the author plus 70 years; works created under a work-made-for-hire arrangement anonymously, or under a pseudonym will have a copyright measured from 120 years from creation or 95 years from publication, whichever occurs first. (see discussion infra regarding Copyright Term Extension Act)

ii. "Architectural works that on the date of enactment are unconstructed and embodied in unpublished plans or drawings." In order to encourage authors of architectural works to construct their unpublished creations, a provisional cut-off date of December 31, 2002, has been provided: works that would ordinarily be eligible for a term of protection continuing past that date will lose protection on the date if the architectural work has not been constructed.

* Works created by individuals. These works will be governed in the first instance by the life plus 70 years *post mortem auctoris* term in § 302 of Title 17, U.S.C.

* Works created under work-made-for-hire. These works will be governed in the first instance by the

term set forth in § 302 of Title 17, U.S.C.: 120 years from the date of creation; the 95 year term for published works made-for-hire will not apply, since the provisions of § 6 of the proposed legislation are limited to architectural works that are unconstructed on the date of enactment.

SOMETHING TO THINK ABOUT:
In general, blueprints and buildings protected together under one copyright.
Must read all sections to understand definition of architectural work (See §§ 206, 101, 102 & Commissioner Reports).
TWO-STEP ANALYSIS

i. Whether original design elements present.
ii. Whether design elements are functionally required. Separability test is not included in Architectural Works section (see Commissioner Report). Instead, use originality requirement and no © protection for standard features.

E. What is not Protected

1. Ideas, systems, processes, discoveries, methods, procedures, or devices as distinguished from a description, explanation or illustration.
2. Works not in a fixed tangible form such as improvisational speeches or performances not in written form.
3. Works containing information that is entirely public domain or common property and containing absolutely no original authorship.
4. Names, phrases, titles, slogans, coloring, or listings of ingredients.

F. Derivative Works and Compilations Under § 103

The fixation and originality requirements apply to all works described by §§ 102(a) and 103(a).

Under § 102, "first generation" works are composed essentially (although not, of course, exclusively) of materials created by their authors.

Under § 103, derivative works and compilations are fundamentally are "second generation" works based on preexisting matter.

So long as the author of a derivative work or compilation incorporates preexisting matter and satisfies both the fixation and originality requirements, the work qualifies for copyright protection under § 103(a).
§ 103(a) states that no copyright can be claimed for any part of a derivative or collective work that has used the pre-existing material unlawfully.
According to § 103(b): The copyright in a compilation or derivative work extends only to the material contributed by the author of such work, as distinguished from the preexisting material employed in the work, and does not imply any exclusive right in the preexisting material. The copyright in such work is independent of, and does not affect or enlarge the scope, duration, ownership, or subsistence of, any copyright protection in the preexisting material.

A "compilations" results from a process of selecting, bringing together, organizing, and arranging previously existing material of all kinds, regardless of whether the individual items in the materials have been or ever could have been subject to copyright.

A "derivative work" requires a process of recasting, transforming, or adapting "one or more preexisting works;" the "preexisting work" must come within the general subject matter of copyright set forth in § 102, regardless of whether it is or was ever copyrighted.

1. Derivative Works.

A derivative work would be an infringement of the work on which it is based. To avoid infringement, the derivative work author of a translation, musical arrangement, or art reproduction must either base his work on one in the public domain or obtain permission from the author of the preexisting copyrighted work. Any recasting, reforming, abridgment, or editorial revision can be copyrighted as a derivative work so long as the standard of originality is met.

Tiffany Design, Inc. v. Reno-Tahoe Specialty, Inc., 55 F. Supp.2d 1113 (D. Nev. 1999) (Tiffany Design created and copyrighted a computer-enhanced image of the Las Vegas strip. Reno-Tahoe Specialty created its own digitally altered photographic image of the Las Vegas Strip. In its production, a Reno-Tahoe employee scanned at least part of a Tiffany Design computer-enhanced photograph of the Las Vegas strip to create a "precursor image." From the precursor image, six architectural works were cut, "manipulated" and placed within the Reno-Tahoe image. The employee claims the image was 85% complete before the Tiffany Design image was even seen.)

The district court found that the act of creating a "precursor image" violated the plaintiff's copyright and awarded partial summary judgment. Such a "precursor image" was a fixed work as soon as it was loaded into the computer's RAM. In deciding the issue of whether the Reno-Tahoe's work violated plaintiff's right to produce derivative works, the court denied summary judgment, finding that there still remained questions of fact as to whether Reno-Tahoe used a substantial amount of the recognizable elements of plaintiff work to constitute "substantial use" (i.e., an infringing derivative work).

Mirage Editions, Inc. v. Albuquerque A.R.T. Co., 856 F.2d 1341 (9th Cir. 1988) (cut out photographs of works of art from a commemorative book and transferred them to individual ceramic tiles.)

OTHER CIRCUITS DO NOT FOLLOW THIS DECISION

The court incorrectly found this to be an infringement of the derivative right , chiefly because defendant's work supplanted the demand for the underlying work. From these facts, it is difficult to understand how the derivative right was infringed. He remounted copies without recasting, transforming, or adapting the copyrighted work in any significant way. This case illustrates a tendency of some courts to push the derivative right beyond reasonable limits to achieve an "equitable" result.

SOMETHING TO THINK ABOUT:

Suppose you cut a Picasso painting into 2000 pieces and resold them. Or suppose that you draw a blue line on a painting that is hanging in your living room. Does either of these acts infringe the copyright?

It does not infringe copyright to resell painting.

Copyright does not cover physical embodiment, but rather it covers expression.

In order to infringe a copyright, there must be an illegal use. You can give child's clothes to a friend but not computer games.

* A copyright exists in both: Fabric Design/Computer Program.

* We want to protect people giving clothes to good will (First Sale Doctrine).

Why is it copyright infringement to copy computer program?
It is okay to use a disk in a computer as long as you don't "copy" it onto hard drive. By copying disk onto hard drive, same thing disk manufacturers do.

First Sale Doctrine (only one use at a time)

* With clothes, only one person can use clothes at a time.
* With computer disk, more than one person can use program at one time.

In the on-line universe, providers want to charge nominal fee to look at information. This knocks down first sale doctrine.

Gracen v. Bradford Exchange, 698 F.2d 300 (7th Cir. 1983) (7th Circuit refused © to an artist's rendering of a photograph of Judy Garland's Dorothy for lack of substantial variation.)
The originality standard, particularly for derivative works such as artistic reproductions, should be higher than for preexisting works, to prevent potential overlapping claims and harassment by claimants of derivative work copyrights. Without requiring a quantum of originality, it may be very difficult to determine whether a third part has copied from a public domain source or copied from the copyrighted work. Thus, too liberal construction of the originality standard may paradoxically inhibit rather than promote the creation of works based on those in the public domain. Therefore, additions to derivative works must be original.

2. Compilations

The compilation differs from the derivative work in one significant way. Unlike the derivative work author, the creator of a compilation does not recast, reform or change the underlying materials but rather compiles (or assembles) them in his own manner. Thus, a compilation can include the selection, coordination, and arrangement of facts, data, or materials that are in the public domain.
Copyright law does not protect facts *per se*, nor the talent that went into discovering them. Rather, copyright protects original works of authorship. One cannot author a fact because facts simply exist, even if they sometimes have to be discovered at

great effort and expense. This principle is embodied in § 102(b) of the 1976 Act which denies copyright to any "discovery, regardless of the form in which it is described. . . ."
A compilation must be independently created and display a de minimis amount of creative, intellectual, or aesthetic labor.

Feist Publications, Inc. v. Rural Telephone Service Co., Inc., 499 U.S. 240, 111 S. Ct. 1282, 113 L. Ed. 358 (1991) (Feist used Rural's telephone listings without permission, copying about 1,300 names and numbers from Rural's white pages, including four fictitious listings that Rural had inserted to detect copying.)

The Supreme Court found that Rural's copyright in its telephone directory did not protect the names and numbers copied by Feist. Constitutional principle that a protectable work must be original with the author. "Original" in the copyright sense means that the work was independently created and possessed at least some minimal degree of creativity. In sum, protection of a factual work extends only to its original selection or arrangement. Thus, even though Feist took a substantial amount of factual information from Rural's directory, it did not take anything that amounted to original authorship. Accordingly, Feist's copying did not constitute copyright infringement.

Feist is unequivocal on one point: an alphabetical listing of telephone subscribers and their numbers cannot be protected as a compilation under copyright unless the selection, coordination, or arrangement of the facts is original.

The Supreme Court specifically discarded industrious effort ("sweat of the brow") as standard for copyrightability separate from the effort's embodiment in the creative arrangement, selection, and coordination of the subject matter in the work.

The yellow pages are a compilation of grouping of ads. Each ad is copyrightable by individual company/ person. If there was no copyright for yellow pages, no incentive to improve the groupings of information. The white pages do not get copyright protection because they are facts. They do not owe their origin to an act of authorship. In addition, originality is a constitutional requirement (can't amend statute to protect facts).

Originality has two parts: SOURCE and CREATIVITY.

"Sweat of the brow" theory no longer exists, only look for originality.

West Publishing Co. v. Mead Data Central, Inc., 799 F.2d 1219 (8th Cir. 1986) (Copyrightability of West's arrangement of legal decisions (the star pagination system) in its National Reporter System; Lexis was not allowed to use star pagination because the arrangement of the cases is copyright and there is originality in the page numbers.)

A numbering system and its factual data are not copyrightable, but the overall arrangement of the actual data is. West does not have copyright protection for the opinions. Lexis wanted to replicate West because it was trying to obtain market control.

The concept of sufficient originality in pagination is very hard to argue (especially after *Feist* which tells us labor and industry are not enough without *modicum* of creativity).

Arguments *West Publishing Co. v. Mead Data Central, Inc.:*
Denying protection - Page numbers are mechanical or accidental.
In favor of protection - West chose cases and designated a unique order. Thus, West did determine or choose the page numbers and this would satisfy the originality requirement.

III. EXCLUSIVE RIGHTS

A. Fundamental Rights

The five fundamental rights given to copyright owners are the exclusive rights of reproduction, adaptation, publication, performance, and display, which is stated generally in § 106.

These exclusive rights, which comprise the so-called "bundle of rights" that is a copyright, are cumulative and may overlap in some cases.

Each of the five enumerated rights may be subdivided indefinitely and may be owned and enforced separately.

Everything in § 106 is made subject to §§ 107-20.

B. Compulsory Licenses

To use a copyrighted work, normally one must obtain from the copyright owner a license whose terms are determined through private bargaining.

In four instances, the Copyright Act supersedes the normal market mechanism for negotiating a license and replaces it with a compulsory license. (Cable television license (§ 111); mechanical license (§ 115); public broadcasting license

(§ 118); and satellite retransmission license (§ 119)).

Under a compulsory license, a third party can use a copyrighted work without the copyright owner's permission, so long as he complies with the statutory procedure and pays the established royalties.

C. Moral Rights

American copyright law is based on the principle that the public benefits by the incentive given to authors to produce copyrighted work. A number of other countries recognize a "moral right" that treats the author's work not as just an economic interest, but rather as an inalienable, natural right and an extension of the artist's personality.
Moral rights are:

i. The right of integrity: the right to insist that the work not be mutilated or distorted;
ii. The right of attribution: the right to be acknowledged as the author of the work and to

prevent others from naming anyone else as the creator; and

iii. The right of disclosure: the right to decide when and in what form the work will be presented to the public.

The concept of moral rights has made its way into American law in three ways:

i. An author's integrity and attribution rights have been protected piecemeal by various bodies of state and federal law;
ii. About a dozen states have passed statutes explicitly recognizing the moral rights of visual artist;
iii. With the Visual Artists Rights Act of 1990, federal law has followed the lead of state law in protecting the integrity and attribution rights of visual artists.

Boosey Hawkes Music Pubs. Ltd. v. Walt Disney Co., 53 U.S.P.Q.2d 2021 (S.D.N.Y. 2000) (Walt Disney Co. and Buena Vista Home Video ("Disney") distributed the Disney video "Fantasia," which includes in its soundtrack a substantial portion of Igor Stravinsky's "Rites of Spring." Boosey, Stravinsky's assignee, argued that such sales infringed Stravinsky's copyright and that the video was "morally offensive," claiming "moral rights damages.")

The court granted Disney's motion in limine to exclude all evidence relating to moral rights. Moral rights are inalienable and unassignable, and thus can only be asserted by the author/composer or his heirs. Therefore, since Boosey is the successor-in-interest to Stravinsky, it did not have standing to bring the claim for moral rights damages.

Gilliam v. American Broadcasting Co., 538 F.2d 14 (2d Cir. 1976) (Plaintiff's right to prevent distortion of his work was protected under both the copyright and unfair competition laws.
ABC obtained a license to broadcast Monty Python program in their entirety except for minor editing to insert commercials. ABC substantially abridged the programs, cutting twenty-four of ninety minutes from them.)
The court held that the unauthorized editing of the underlying work constituted an infringement of the copyright by creating an unauthorized derivative work. Thus, a prospective user of a copyrighted work should negotiate, in the appropriate situation, a

license to adapt, as well as the rights to reproduce and perform, the work.
Court should have said no right to make derivative work was passed on and that would have been the end of the case.

This case has never been followed.

SOMETHING TO THINK ABOUT:
Statute defines copyright owner's rights:
- In 1909 Act, copyright in certain works, can assign rights, can make copies.
- In 1976 Act, § 106(2) grants the right to control derivative works.

Moral rights run against private property law (Congress viewed it as alien to give someone something with condition attached that will come back in 10 years to check on it).

Suppose you make a sculpture and sell to John Smith. John takes sculpture apart into 3 pieces. Can you sue?
NO - Under the first sale doctrine, John can do what he wants with it.

Suppose you sell picture to hotel, but tell the hotel that it must not frame or change lighting. Can you enforce contract?
YES - Can give partial ©.

Wojnarowicz v. American Family Association, 745 F. Supp. 130 (S.D.N.Y. 1990)
This case deals with New York law, not VARA.
The New York Artists' Authorship Rights Act prevents unauthorized public display, publication, or reproduction of an altered, defaced or mutilate work where such display would reasonably damage the artist's reputation. The New York Art provides that "the artist shall retain at all times the right to claim authorship." While one violates the New York Act by displaying the defaced art work (focuses on the artist's reputational interest), one violates the California Act by defacing a work of art (emphasizes a broad personal interest in the integrity of cultural preservation). Both statutes are limited in their application to works of fine art. These state moral right acts present serious questions of federal preemption under § 301 of the Copyright Act and the Visual Artists Rights Act of 1990.
One has the right to criticize an author's work under the First Amendment, but to get out of problem would be to add language to say it's only a portion of work.

Court awarded nominal damages of $1.

D. The Visual Artists Rights Act of 1990 (VARA) § 106A

The VARA protects both the reputations of certain visual artists and the works of art they create. It provides these artists with the rights of "attribution" and "integrity."
These rights are analogous to those protected by Article 6 of the Berne Convention, which are commonly know as "moral rights."
Only the author of the work of visual art can claim protection (whether or not artist is copyright owner).
Work made for hire not included.
§ 106A(a)(3)(A) Mutilation that is prejudicial to his or her honor or reputation that is intentional.
§ 106A(a)(3)(B) Intentional or grossly negligent destruction of work.
§ 504 Only give statutory damages for VARA
§ 501 Can get an injunction? (But work is already destroyed what good would it do?).
The point of VARA is to act as window dressing to comply with Berne Convention. Moral rights are inevitable. Moral rights are being diluted in Europe instead of being built in USA.

Summary of Provisions of Visual Artists Rights Act of 1990
The major provisions of the Act are:

1. **Works protected**. The Act does not cover all possible visual art works, but instead is limited to works of visual art. Qualified works include paintings, drawings, prints, sculptures and still photographic images produced for exhibition purposes only, and existing in single copies or in limited editions of 200 or fewer copies, signed by the artist. Works not covered include reproductions of qualifying works and works destined for commercial purpose. Works made for hire are excluded specifically.
(§ 101, "work of visual art").

2. **Rights of attribution and integrity**. The rights of attribution includes the artist's rights:
   a. to claim authorship of the work;
   b. to prevent the use of her name as the author of any work of visual art which she did not create; and

c. to prevent the use of her name as the author of the work in the event of a distortion, mutilation or other modification of the work which would be prejudicial to her honor or reputation.

(§106A(a), "recognized stature" has been defined in the case law as describing a work that is meritorious and acknowledged as such by art experts and other member of the artistic community, or by some cross-section of society.)

3. **Scope and exercise of rights**. The author of a work of visual art has the rights provided in § 106A, whether or not she owns the copyright in the work and whether or not the work qualifies for protection under the national origin provisions of § 104. (§ 106A(b)).

   Exceptions. There are three exceptions:

   i. A work is not destroyed, distorted, mutilated or otherwise objectionably modified, for purposes of the integrity right, if the modification is the result of the passage of time or the inherent nature of the materials;
   ii. The integrity right is not violated when a modification is the result of conservation measures or of public presentation, including lighting or placement, unless the modification is caused by gross negligence; and
   iii. The integrity and attribution rights do not apply to reproductions or other uses of protected works in forms not themselves protected by VARA. (§106A(c)).

4. **Removal of works from buildings**. The Act amends § 113 to establish conditions under which a work of art incorporated as a part of a building may be removed from the building. If the work cannot be removed without being mutilated or destroyed, the owner of the building can remove if the artist consented to the installation before June 1, 1991, or if thereafter she consented to the eventuality of mutilation or destruction in a signed instrument. If work can be removed without mutilation or destruction, the work automatically is subject to the artist's attribution and integrity rights unless the owner has tried and failed to notify

the artist. If notice succeeds, the artist has 90 days to remove the work or pay for its removal. (§ 113(d)).

5. **Duration of rights**. With respect to works of visual art created on or after June 1, 1991, the effective date of the Act, the § 106A rights endure for the life of the artist. If the work of visual art was created before June 1, 1991 and the artist has not parted with title to the copy/copies of the work, the artist receives the life-plus-70-years term for both the § 106 rights and the § 106A rights. If the work was created before June 1, 1991 and the artist has sold the copy/copies to others, no §106A rights arise at all. § 106A(d)).

6. **Transfer and waiver.** The artist's attribution and integrity rights cannot be transferred.

7. **Infringement**. The Act subjects violators of the new attribution and integrity rights in works of visual art to the normal liabilities for infringement, but not to criminal penalties. (§§ 501, 506).

8. **Preemption**. The statute amends § 301 by preempting any legal or equitable rights at state law that are equivalent to those created by the Act's new provisions. (§ 301(f)).

SOMETHING TO THINK ABOUT:

Suppose you take photos in the Forbes Museum and hang them in a gallery with 'X's over them. Can Forbes sue you?
NO - Not under VARA because didn't mutilate original.
Also, not know if work considered a visual art.
Destroying photo not a problem. § 106A(c)(3)

Suppose you go into the Forbes Museum and draw 'X's on the original paintings. Does author have claim against you?

i. Need to know if artist still alive? § 106A(d) (right endures for *life* of artist)
ii. Need to be a work of recognized stature (but recognized by whom?) § 106A(a)(3)(B) this is a major limitation on the statute.
iii. Was it intentional? Did it hurt reputation?

If you destroy it, you mutilate it.
If you mutilate it, you may not have destroyed it.

IV. OWNERSHIP AND TRANSFERS

When thinking about ownership and transfers of rights, asks and answers the following questions: Who owns the copyright in the work, once created, and how is ownership transferred by persons, subsequent to the initial owner, who are interested in exploiting the copyright?

Two Basic Principles

i. Mere ownership of a copy or phonorecord does not give the owner a copyright.
ii. Minors may claim copyright protection, but state laws may regulate dealings with minors.

A. Initial Ownership

Initial ownership of copyright is easy to determine when an individual creates a work at his own instance and expense. However, many works are created as the result of an employment relationship ("work made for hire", in the language of the 1976 Act) or through the combined efforts of several persons ("joint works").

Initial Ownership

Two basic and well-established principles of copyright law are restated in § 201(a): that the source of the copyright ownership is the author or the work, and that, in the case of a "joint work," the co-authors of the work are likewise co-owners of the copyright.

Under § 101, a work is "joint" if the authors collaborated with each other, or if each of the authors prepared his or her contribution with the knowledge and intention that it would be merged with the contributions of other authors as "inseparable or interdependent parts of a unitary whole." The touchstone here is the intention, at the writing is done, that the parts be absorbed or combined into an integrated unit, although the parts themselves may be either "inseparable" or "interdependent."

Work made for hire

§ 201(b): In the case of works made for hire, the employer is considered the author or the work and is regarded as the initial owner of copyright unless there has been an agreement otherwise. Any agreement under which the employee is to own rights must be in writing and signed by the parties.

The basic problem is how to draw a statutory line between those works written on special order or commission that should be considered as "works made for hire" and those that should not.

Contributions to collective works
§ 201(c) deals with the troublesome problem of ownership of copyright in contributions to collective works, and the relationship between copyright ownership in a contribution and in the collective work in which it appears.

* Under § 101, a "collective work" is a species of "compilation" and, by its nature, must involve the selection, assembly, and arrangement of "a number of contributions."
* Unlike the contents of other types of "compilations," each of the contributions incorporated in a "collective work" must itself constitute a "separate and independent" work, therefore ruling out compilations of information or other uncopyrightable material and works published with editorial revisions or annotations.

The second sentence of § 201(c), in conjunction with the provisions of § 404 dealing with copyright notice, will preserve the author's copyright in a contribution even if the contribution does not bear a separate notice in the author's name, and without requiring any unqualified transfer of rights to the owner of the collective work.

1. Works Made for Hire

In order to be considered a work made for hire:

i. Employee within scope of employment or work ordered or commissioned for use as a collective work, as a translation, as part of a motion picture, as an atlas, as a compilation, or as a test.
ii. Full time employee;
iii. No agreement needs to be signed to get this;
iv. This can be altered in writing separate agreement.

Therefore, employee will negotiate for employer to assign back rights in a work which he creates.
Employer now is the author, not the employee.

Before *Community for Creative Non-violence v. Reid*, the issue which has divided the case law is whether the clause "employee within the scope of his or her employment" in subdivision (1) can encompass an independent contractor in some circumstances.

Two views emerged:

i. Broadly reading statute to include independent contractor; or
ii. Narrowly reading statute, limiting it to the master-servant relationship in agency law.

Neither "employee" nor "independent contractor" is defined by the 1976 Act.

Community For Creative Non-Violence v. Reid, 490 U.S. 730, 109 S. Ct. 2166, 104 L. Ed. 2d 811 (1989)
The Supreme Court limited the definition of employee in subdivision (1) to the master-servant relationship as understood by the common law of agency.
A charitable organization dedicated to eliminating homelessness claimed copyright ownership of a statute called "Third World America." CCNV had commissioned the sculptor, Reid, to create a sculpture dramatizing the plight of the homeless for a Christmas pageant in Washington, D.C. CCNV supplied the plans and sketches, ultimately executed by Reid. On that basis, CCNV claimed ownership of the copyright in the sculpture as an employer for hire. The Supreme Court ruled for Reid and found that the work could not be a work made for hire.

Four bases for a work made for hire emerged in the case law:

i. A work made for hire comes into existence when the hiring party retains the right to control the work;
ii. A work made for hire comes into existence when the hiring party actually retains control in the creation of the work;
iii. The term "employee" applies only to those persons so defined under agency law; and
iv. The term "employee" only refers to formal salaried employees.

After *CCNV*, contractual arrangements creating a work made for hire are more difficult. Employers will adopt a rule of thumb: when in doubt, insist on an assignment of copyright from the prospective employee. Although an assignment of copyright provides a somewhat shorter duration of copyright ownership than a work made for hire, it may satisfy the

needs of most employers. Grants of rights in works for hire, unlike most other types of grants (an assignment can be terminated between the thirty-fifth and fortieth years of the grant), are immune from termination by operation of law under the provisions of the current statute. §§ 203 and 304(c).
The Court looked at the statute as follows:
§ 201(b): It is possible for employer to give back some rights to employee.
§ 101(a)(1) ("work made for hire"): If Reid is an employee, then it is work made for hire.
§ 101(a)(2) ("work made for hire"): Not applicable as commission work for hire since not a signed agreement which you need.

CCNV paid salary, gave much direction, control, supervision and generated the idea, concept and analysis of the work. Thus, under an instance and expense test, *CCNV* argued that the court should consider the reason for creation and the financial backing for the creation. Also, it stated that because it paid Reid's taxes and benefits, he should be afforded full-time employer status.
Court stated that if you fail categories of commission work, you cannot then claim employee status. Court used commonly understood definition of employee. Thus, if statute uses a work defined in another statute and commonly understood, then that is definition if same basic context.

SOMETHING TO THINK ABOUT:
Why not use Ninth Circuit approach?
Court is supposed to interpret a statute. Nothing in legislative history or language gives that interpretation. Court is not Congress. Therefore, it cannot make such a decision. The courts role is to only interpret the law, not make new law. If legislature wants this, then they can pass this legislation.
If legislative history is unclear about definition, court will look to common understanding of word.

"Work made for hire" is statutorily created status.

Do we need "Work Made for Hire" and why?

We don't know as an empirical matter. As a theoretical matter, "work made for hire" creates incentive and is risk taking (Who is in better position; MARKET v. WORK).
The larger the company, the more conservative and less variety.

Why not decide case as a joint work?
CCNV contributed ideas, but this was not enough. Even though *CCNV* had the idea and the money, it should not protect this because Reid is an artist and his work should be protected.
Two competing views:

i. Economic - protect investors: Work made for hire.
ii. If want to leave property right with author: Joint work.

Suppose a screenwriter was able to get an interview with a criminal defendant and writes a screenplay about his trial. The production studio happy to look at the script as long as it is "Work Made for Hire." What would you say if you were the screenwriter?
You don't like it.
Under § 101(1), you are not an employee.
Under § 101(2), Is this a commissioned work?

i. Fulfilled one of seven required works (movie).
ii. Must sign an agreement.

Problem is with commission definition. Possible definition is authorization to perform certain act (commission sale - % of profits).
Courts hold that timing doesn't matter (except for one district). Work is commissioned if satisfy required work and signed agreement.

2. Joint Works

§ 101 defines a "joint work" as a work prepared by two or more authors with the intention that their contributions by merged into inseparable or interdependent parts of a unitary whole. What counts is that the authors intended their respective labors to be integrated into one work. The contributions of the individual authors do not have to be equal in quantity and quality.

Courts have unanimously denied joint authorship claims where an individual contribution is not itself copyrightable. Thus, a joint author must not only intend that his contribution be part of a joint work but must contribute more than *de minimus* authorship to the resulting work.

Why this insistence upon copyrightable contributions from all joint authors?

i. Seems more consistent with the spirit of copyright law.
ii. Prevents spurious claims by those who might otherwise try to share the fruits of the efforts of a sole author; and
iii. It may encourage those with non-copyrightable contributions to protect heir rights through contract, because if they neglect to do so, the copyright will remain with the one or more persons who created the copyrightable material.

Childress v. Taylor, 945 F.2d 500 (2d Cir. 1991)
(The defendant Taylor contacted Childress to write a play based on the life of the legendary comedienne "Moms" Mabley. Although Taylor, a professional actress, wrote none of the script, she provided Childress with her research of "Moms" Mabley's life, and suggested that certain scenes be included in the play. The relationship between the two parties deteriorated before the rights were specified by contract. Taylor then had another author modify the script and shortly thereafter, using this new version, she performed the work publicly. In response to Childress's suit for copyright infringement, Taylor contended she was a joint author and shared with Childress the rights to the play.)
The Second Circuit rejected Taylor's claim of joint authorship because her efforts lacked the two basic elements needed to create a joint work. First, she only supplied ideas and research, and did not contribute the requisite degree of authorship. Second, even if Taylor's contribution was independently copyrightable, a joint work was not created due to a lack of intent.
One needs intent to be joint authors to avoid slippery slope (i.e., Overhearing someone talking about a dog on the subway and writing a story about it).
Circuits are split as to whether each contribution must be copyrightable. The Supreme Court has not answered question yet.

SOMETHING TO THINK ABOUT
What is profit division of joint work?
Under § 201(a), authors of joint work are co-authors of copyright in their work.

* Each gets half.
* Each has power to contract with 3rd party for entire work without consent of co-author.

3. Collective Works
According to § 101, a "collective work" is a work, such as a periodical issue, anthology, or encyclopedia, in which a number of contributions, constituting separate and independent works in themselves, are assembled into a collective whole.
Unlike other types of compilations, however, a collective work consists of separate and independent works capable of copyright themselves.
Under § 201(c), one should distinguish copyright in the contribution to the collective work from copyright in the collective work.
The individual contributors to the collective work retain the copyrights in their works, absent a written agreement stating the contrary.

B. Transfer of Rights

Ownership of Copyright
Under § 201(d)(1), the ownership of a copyright, or of any part of it, may be transferred by any means of conveyance or by operation of law, and is to be treated as personal property upon the death of the owner.

The term "transfer of copyright ownership" is defined in § 101 to cover any "conveyance, alienation, or hypothecation, including assignment, mortgages, and exclusive licenses, but not including nonexclusive licenses. . . ."

§ 201(d)(2) recognizes the principle of divisibility of copyright. The principle of divisibility applies whether or not the transfer is "limited in time or place of effect." The term "copyright owner," with respect to any one exclusive right, refers to the owner of that particular right and is entitled "to all of the protection and remedies accorded to the copyright owner."

§ 201(e) provides that when an individual author's ownership or a copyright have not previously been voluntarily transferred, no action by any governmental body or other official or organization purporting to seize, expropriate, transfer, or exercise rights of ownership with respect to the copyright, or any exclusive rights under a copyright, shall be given effect under this title. . . ."

Distinction Between Ownership of Copyright and Material Object
Copyright ownership and ownership of a material object in which the copyrighted work is embodied are entirely separate things.

1. Execution and Recordation of Transfers

Under § 204(a), a transfer of copyright ownership is valid only if there exists an instrument of conveyance, or alternatively a "note or memorandum or the transfer," which is in writing and signed by the copyright owner " or such owner's duly authorized agent."

§ 204(b) makes clear that a notarial or consular acknowledgment is not essential to the validity of any transfer, whether executed in the United States or abroad.

§ 205(c) makes clear that the recorded document will give constructive notice of its contents only if two conditions are met:

i. The document or attached material specifically identifies the work to which it pertains sot that a reasonable search under the title or registration number would reveal it, and
ii. Registration has been made for the work.

Under § 205(c), a nonexclusive license in writing and signed, whether recorded or not, would be valid against a later transfer, and would also prevail as against a prior unrecorded transfer if taken in good faith and without notice.

The Bundle of Rights
A copyright is independent of both its physical manifestation and the very thing that is copyrighted.
Under the 1909 Act, a copyright was perceived as an indivisible bundle of rights incapable of being broken up into smaller rights and exercised by multiple owners.
Under the 1976 Act, however, there is an explicit statutory recognition of the principle of divisibility of copyrights.

Effects Associates v. Cohen, 908 F.2d 555 (9th Cir. 1990)
The writing requirement is a flexible one, it must be signed by the copyright owner. Although the "writing" may take many forms, it can be viewed as a simple, straightforward, and absolute requirement for a valid transfer of copyright. Accordingly, courts have not relaxed the writing requirement to allow for industry practices (movie industry), where written contracts are not the way business is done.

SOMETHING TO THINK ABOUT:

If you have a writing, look at § 101 ("transfer of © ownership").
Under § 204, transfer (definition in § 101) not valid unless in writing. You would get exclusive right.
Court next looks at a non-exclusive license to use plaintiff's special effects footage.
§ 101 - explicitly excludes non-exclusive license.
§ 202(d)(1) - Can transfer it anyway you want.
If you don't want exclusive rights, may get non-exclusive rights without writing. Look at:
Language of statute, legislative history, case law, treatises, and industry practice (prevalent at time of act & case).
§ 205 gives you a hint that non-exclusive license may be not in writing.
Thus, copyright rights are only as good as your written agreement. Need to look at whether parties have power to negotiate. Work made for hire must be written (in statute), unless you are an employee.

Cohen v. Paramount Pictures Corp., 845 F.2d 851 (9th Cir. 1988)
Example of the stricter approach to construing contractual language, one that would take a more literal reading of the contractual terms.
The issue was whether a license conferring the right to exhibit a film "by means of television" included the right to distribute videocassettes of the film. When executed in 1969, the videocassette was not envisaged.
The court found for Cohen (who wished to prevent distribution of the videocassettes). The court scrutinized the contractual terms of the Cohen-Paramount license and found that it lacked broad enough language to encompass distribution by videocassette (other contracts included language like "the right to exhibit films by methods yet to be invented"). The purposes of

the Act would be frustrated if the court construed this license with its limiting language as granting a right in a medium that had not been introduced to the domestic market at the time the parties entered into the agreement.

C. Recordation

§ 205 permits recordation in the Copyright Office of all documents of copyright ownership, whether assignment, exclusive licenses, or nonexclusive licenses. To enjoy fully the benefits of the 1976 Act, an owner of any such interest should accompany the recordation with a registration of the subject work, if it is not already registered.

What should be recorded?

§ 204(a) provides that a transfer of ownership may be accomplished by a signed "instrument of conveyance, or a note or memorandum of the transfer."

Why record?

For causes of action arising before March 1, 1989, recordation of a copyright interest is a prerequisite to bringing a suit for copyright infringement.

For causes of action arising on or after March 1, 1989, recordation is no longer required as a prerequisite to bring a copyright infringement suit. However, it is highly recommended.

Also, recordation establishes priority of ownership between conflicting transfers of copyright, as well as between conflicting transfers and nonexclusive licenses.

Priority between conflicting transfers

Under § 205(d), if A transfers a copyright to B, and then later to C (C takes without knowledge), the first to record owns the copyright. However, the transferee has a one-month grace period (two-month if outside country) to record from the date of execution of the agreement.

These priority rules apply only if the work is registered in addition to being recorded.

Priority between transfers and nonexclusive licenses

Under § 205(e), a nonexclusive license will prevail over an assignment or exclusive license if:

i. The nonexclusive license must be evidenced in a written instrument signed by the copyright owner and have been take before execution of the transfer; and

ii. If the nonexclusive license was taken after the transfer, it will prevail if it is evidence in writing and was taken in good faith before recordation of the transfer without notice thereof.

V. DURATION OF COPYRIGHT

How long does ownership endure?

1790 Act: 14 years + 14 years (if author survives to end).
1909 Act: 28 years + 28 years.
1976 Act: Life + 70 years.
Work made for hire = 120 years from creation or 95 years from publication whichever shorter (also anonymous & pseudonymous works).

Note, effective October 27, 1998, under the Sonny Bono Copyright Term Extension Act, copyright terms were extended by 20 years.
Also note, this legislation does not restore copyright protection to any works that are in the public domain.

SOMETHING TO THINK ABOUT:
Why under the 1909 Act is the term 28 + 28 years instead of 56 years?

i. Will fall into public domain faster.
ii. Bridging the gap.
iii. Second bite at the apple theory (If didn't get much money in first 28 years, can renegotiate). A lot of people create works that are underrated initially didn't know value when it first came out.
iv. Argument only works if renegotiation after 28 years.

TERMINATION RIGHTS are a recodification of the second bite at the apple from 1909 Act.

A. Duration and Renewal

It is impossible to determine the minimum duration sufficient to encourage the optimum amount of investment for the enormous range and variety or works of authorship.

A copyright term consists of the life of the author and 70 years after his death. Under the 1909 Act, protection begins on the date of publication (registration for unpublished works) and continues for 28 years from that date; it may be renewed for a second 28 years, making a total of 56 years.

Arguments for changing this system to one based on the life of the author:

i. The present 56-year term is not long enough to insure an author and his dependents the fair economic benefits from his works.
ii. The tremendous growth in communications media has substantially lengthened the commercial life of a great many works.
iii. Although limitations on the term of copyright are obviously necessary, too short a term harms the author without giving any substantial benefit to the public.
iv. A system based on the life of the author would go a long way toward clearing up the confusion and uncertainty involved in the vague concept of "publication," and would provide a much simpler, clearer method for computing the term.
v. One of the worst features of the present copyright law is the provision for renewal of copyright. Under a life-plus-70 system the renewal device would be inappropriate and unnecessary.
vi. Under the preemption provisions of § 301 and the single Federal system they would establish, authors will be giving up perpetual, unlimited exclusive common law rights in their unpublished works, including works that have been widely disseminated by means other than publication.
vii. A very large majority of the world's countries have adopted a copyright term of the life of the author and 50 years after the author's death. Since American authors are frequently protected longer in foreign countries than in the United States, the disparity in the duration of copyright has provoked considerable resentment and some proposals for retaliatory legislation. A change in the basis of our copyright term would place the United States in the forefront of the international copyright community.

The advantages of a basic term of copyright enduring for the life of the author and for 70 years after the author's death outweigh any possible disadvantages.

B. Basic copyright term

Under § 302(a), a work "created" on or after the effective date of the revised statute would be protected by statutory copyright "from its creation" and, with exceptions, "endures for a term consisting of the life of the author and 70 years after the author's death."

1. Joint works

Since by definition a "joint work" has two or more authors, the term of copyright is measured from the death of the last survivors of a group of joint authors, no matter how many there are. Therefore, under the Sonny Bono Copyright Term Extension Act, the copyright will endure for 70 years after the last surviving joint author's death.

2. Anonymous works, pseudonymous works, and works made for hire

§ 302(c) provides a special term for anonymous works, pseudonymous works, and works made for hire: 95 years from publication or 120 years from creation, whichever expires first.

§ 302(c) provides that the 95- and 120-year terms for an anonymous or pseudonymous work can be converted to the ordinary life-plus-70 term if "the identity of one or more authors . . . is revealed" in special records maintained for this purpose in the Copyright Office.
The alternative terms established in § 302(c), 95 years from publication or 120 years from creation, whichever expires first, are necessary to set a time limit on protection of unpublished material.

3. Records and presumption as to author's death

§ 302(d) and (e) together furnish an answer to practical problems of how to discover the death dates of obscure or unknown authors.

4. Preexisting Works under Common Law Protection

Every "original work of authorship" fixed in tangible form that is in existence would be given statutory copyright protection as long as the work is not in the public domain in this country.

§ 303 provides protection for works created but not published or registered before January 1, 1978. § 303 provides that under no circumstances would copyright protection expire before December 31, 2002. The copyright term will not expire before December 31, 2047 (this provides for 45 years of more protection - - 25 years plus 20 years as a result of the Sonny Bono Copyright Term Extension Act). This also attempts to encourage to encourage publication by providing 25 years more protection (through 2027) if the work were published before the end of 2002.

5. Duration of Subsisting Copyrights

The statute's approach is to increase the present 56-year term to **95** years in the case of copyrights subsisting in both their first and their renewal terms.

The total term has been extended to **95** years (previously 75 years) from the date the copyright was secured as a result of the Sonny Bono Copyright Term Extension Act.

6. Copyrights in their first term

§ 304(a) reenacts and preserves the renewal provision, previously in § 24 of the statute, for all works presently in their first 28-year term. Renewal registration will be required during the 28th year of the copyright but the length of the renewal term will be increased from 28 to 47 years. Under the most recent Sonny Bono Copyright Term Extension Act, the total term is extended to 95 years from the date the copyright was secured

7. Copyrights in their renewal term

Renewal copyrights that are subsisting in their second term at any time during the period between December 31, 1976 and December 31, 1977, inclusive, would be extended under

§ 304(b) to run for a total of 95 years. This provision would add another 19 years to the duration of any renewed copyright whose second term started during the 28 years immediately preceding the effective date of the act

(January 1, 1978).
§ 304(b) also extends the duration of renewal copyrights whose second 28-year term is scheduled to expire during 1977.

§ 304(b) also covers the special situation of a subsisting first-term copyright that becomes eligible for renewal registration during the year before the act comes into effect.

If a renewal registration is not made before the effective date, the case is governed by the provisions of § 304(a).

If a renewal registration is made during the year before the new law takes effect, however, the copyright would be treated as if it were already existing in its second term and would be extended to the full period of 95 years without the need for further renewal.

Provided the work did not fall into the public domain prior to October 27, 1998, the total copyright term is extended to 95 years from date copyright is secured.

8. Year End Expirations of Terms

Under § 305, the term of copyright protection for a work extends through December 31 of the year in which the term would otherwise have expired.
§ 305 applies only to "terms of copyright provided by

§§ 302- 04," which are sections dealing with duration of copyright.

Since all copyright terms under the bill expire on December 31, and since § 304(a) requires that renewal be made "within one year prior to the expiration of the original term of copyright," the period for renewal registration in all cases will run from December 31 through December 31 at the ending year.

Fred Fisher Music Co. v. Witmark & Sons, 318 U.S. 643, 63. S. Ct. 773, 87 L. Ed. 1055 (1943)

The Supreme Court held that an assignment by an author of the renewal term, before that right had vested, was binding on the author. It soon became industry practice to require an assignment of the author's renewal rights in the initial contract.

In order to sell their works, authors were pressured into conveying their renewal rights in the second copyright term. The renewal rights may be assigned before their vesting, whereby the right to terminate cannot be assigned away in advance.

SOMETHING TO THINK ABOUT:

In *Fred fisher Music Co.,* the heirs were not parties to the contract.
If the author is living at the time of the renewal, the author will not get a second bite at the apple (compensated for consideration).
If the author is dead at the time of renewal, heirs should get second bite at the apple (won't know value of work for years 29 - 56).
Fred Fisher Music Co. appears to have been decided incorrectly because it is contrary to the second bite at the apple. If meant second bite at the apple, author can't reassign rights until renewal term. To get around second bite at the apple, owner could name an heir as an assignee.

The renewal provision adds 28 years to those who make the effort (renegotiate and go back to the Copyright Office).

To get U.S. closer to world market:

* Protection from time fixed.
* Rights inherent for doing work (don't have to do anything to receive rights).
* Still have problem for unrealized gain.

Epoch Producing Corp. v. Killiam Shows, Inc., 522 F.2d 737 (2d Cir. 1975)
Demonstrates some of the difficulties involved in the retroactive application to determine who, is anyone, owns the renewal term in a copyrighted work.

Plaintiff Epoch asserted ownership as an employer for hire of Griffith's Birth of a Nation, and argued that is had the right to claim the renewal term in the work. Epoch had renewed the work in 1942 and brought its suit for infringement against Killiam in 1969. The defendant argued that Epoch had no right to claim the renewal term because it did not qualify as an employer for hire. Thus, according the defendant, the work had entered the public domain because it had not been renewed by the proper party.

The court agreed that no work for hire was created and that, unlike an original registration of copyright, a renewal registration carried no presumption of validity. In addition, Griffith nowhere explicitly stated his intent to convey the renewal right. Thus, the work had entered the public domain after the first 28-year term of copyright.

SOMETHING TO THINK ABOUT:
Is there a writing?
YES - Look at intent of the parties.

i. "All its right, title and interest" and "for the term of 28-years."
ii. "Copyright acquired by it by public presentation for the motion picture photoplay."

If renewal term not explicit in terms, it does not pass. Author must contract right out in order to get second bite at the apple.

Why not allow assignee to hold renewal unless author decides otherwise?

i. Author should get second bite of apple because intellectual property gains value over time and author should get benefit.
ii. Changes burden of proof.
iii. Uneven bargaining power (want to read contract against party who had superior bargaining power or drafter).

9. Copyright Term Extension Act (Sonny Bono Act)

Effective October 27, 1998, under the Copyright Term Extension Act (Sonny Bono Act), copyright terms were extended by 20 years. This applies to all existing works currently protected by copyright on the effective date. It does not, however, restore copyright protection to any work that are in the public domain.

Eldred v. Reno, 239 F.3d 372 (D.C. Cir. 2001) (Copyright Term Extension Act of 1998 (CTEA) retroactively lengthened the terms of copyrights. Plaintiffs asserted that CTEA violated the First Amendment as well as the "originality" and "limited times" constitutional requirements.)

The D.C. Circuit Court of Appeals determined that neither the First Amendment nor the Copyright Clause prohibits Congress from changing the duration of existing copyrights. While the court upheld familiar idea/expression doctrine, the Court did not find any First Amendment right to commercially use the works of others. Regarding the "originality" challenge, the Court determined that existing copyrights do not have to re-satisfy the originality requirement to be extended. The Court also rejected the "limited times" argument pointing out that the preamble "is not a substantive limit" on Congress' power. Therefore, the statutory extension of copyright duration was not unconstitutional and the decision dismissing plaintiffs' action was affirmed.

10. Summary of Copyright Terms

Date of Work	Copyright Term
Published before 1923	Work in the public domain
Published 1923-1963 Properly renewed Never renewed	 95 years from publication Work in the public domain
Published 1964-1977	95 years from publication
Created before 1978, but not published or registered	Life + 70 years, but will not expire before Dec. 31, 2002 (if published before end of 2002, will not expire before Dec. 31, 2002)
Created 1978 or later (whether or not published)	Life + 70 years (if work-made-for-hire/ anonymous/ pseudonymous: 120 years from creation or 95 years from publication, whichever shorter)

C. COPYRIGHT RENEWAL ACT OF 1992

***Permissive renewal*:** For works whose copyright was secured between 1964 and 1977, the Renewal Act confers renewal automatically when the first term ends. On the other hand, pre-1964 works are not affected by the 1992 legislation.

***Clarifying the vesting date*:** If a renewal application is filed during the 28th year by the person entitled to the renewal, the renewal term will vest, at the beginning of the 29th year, in that person, even if that person dies before the renewal term begins. If no application is made, the renewal term will vest in whoever is the appropriate renewal claimant on December 31st of the initial term's 28th year.

The incentive to register: Thanks to automatic renewal, the renewal term will no longer be lost for failure to comply with renewal formalities. If a timely renewal is filed, the author's first-term grants of renewal rights to exploit such derivative works are nullified if the author dies before the renewal term. If registration is made during the last year of the first term, the certificate of renewal registration shall constitute *prima facie* evidence as to the validity of the facts stated in the certificate. Remedies for copyright infringement are narrowed for authors who fail to file a timely renewal registration and disallows statutory and actual damages, attorney's fees, and seizure and forfeiture (§§ 504, 505, and 509) for all infringements that commence before registration.

***Stewart v. Abend*,** 495 US 207, 110 S. Ct. 1750, 109 L. Ed. 2d 184 (1990)

The Supreme Court held that the assignment of renewal rights by an author does not defeat the right of the author's statutory successor(s) to those rights if the author dies before the renewal right vests. In other words, when the grant or rights in the preexisting work lapses, the right to use parts of it in the derivative work ceases, and its continued use will infringe the preexisting work. This case involved the film right to a short story, first published in 1942. The author, Woolrich, assigned the film rights to the short story to a production company and agreed to renew the copyright and assign the rights to the second term. Stewart and Hitchcock acquired theses rights and released the film version, Rear Window, in 1954. Woolrich died in 1968 before he could renew his copyright. In the 1969, the executor of Woolrich's estate renewed the copyright and assigned the renewal term to Abend. On the re-release of the film in various media, Abend sued for copyright infringement, claiming that the right to use the film version terminated when Woolrich died before renewing the copyright.

The Supreme Court agreed with Abend, holding that the derivative work film could not be exploited without the permission of the owner of the underlying work. One may exploit only such copyrighted material as one owns or is authorized to use. Under this principle, a derivative work author cannot escape his obligations to the owner of the renewal copyright merely because he created a new version under an assignment or license that ended with the first copyright term.

Simply stated, Stewart denies continued exploitation during the renewal term of derivative work prepared during the initial term, unless rights during the renewal term were properly obtained. Of course, the derivative work author owns the original elements added to the underlying work and can continue to use them as he wished, unless this use would infringe the underlying work.

If no registration is filed, a derivative work made pursuant to the grant can still be exploited but no new derivative work can be made after the new term begins.

If the renewal right vests in the author (author is alive at the renewal time), he is bound by the grant, and the assignee will own the renewal rights.

If the author dies before renewal vest, the author's statutory beneficiaries can prevent the assignee from exploiting the derivative work, but only if renewal registration is timely claimed.

Without timely renewal registration, an authorized derivative work prepared under the grant can continue to be exploited under the terms of the grant.

The renewal term creates an entirely new right, one that reverts automatically to the author and his family, unencumbered by assignment and licenses granted during the initial term. This suggest that a license to prepare a derivative work would terminate at the end of the initial term, as would the right to exploit the derivative work prepared under that license.

A derivative work may be individually copyrighted, and the derivative work author will own the copyright in the original elements added to the underlying work.

SOMETHING TO THINK ABOUT:

Can Abend prevent the showing of rear window?
Majority theory: Rights in original work supersede any rights in derivative works. This case was decided under § 7 of the 1909 Act.
Under 1976 Act, Rear Window may be viewed (§ 203(b)(1), § 304(c)(6)(A)).

To prevent case, Stewart should have kept track of renewal and outbid Abend. Abend did not want to prevent viewing, he merely wanted money.
Courts are unhappy about suppressing and enjoining creative works. They would rather award money because they don't want to be responsible for works not shown.

Suppose created and published work in 1954 (pre-'78, first term). When does it fall into public domain?
Look at 1909 Act.
First 28 years end in 1982.
* Work first term end after 1978.
* Renewal term of 67 years (§ 304(a)(1)(B)(ii)) plus Copyright Term Extension Act (additional 20 years)

What if assign renewal term (28 year)?
§ 304(c)(3) - After 56 years, have 5 year window to terminate. (Third bite at the apple).
Cannot contract to not terminate (§ 304(c)(5)).
Default position is assignee holds copyright until end of 67 years unless author takes action.

Suppose created and published work in 1940 (pre-'78 renewal term). When does it fall into public domain?
Go to 1968 in first term and then renew in second term in 1978.
§ 304(b) Extended to endure for term of 95 years from date © was originally secured (1940).

§ 304(c) Work in first or renewal term author gets benefit of extended term.

Only author, children, widow and grandchildren can terminate (not assignees).
Any work in existence after 1978, covered by 1976 Act (incorp. part of 1909 Act) [Stewart is a 1909 Act case because the renewal occurred before 1978 and the case was questioning the renewal.]
Works are distinguished between first term, renewal term, or work not in existence as of January 1, 1978. (§ 303 © work created but not published or © before January 1, 1978.)

Starting in 1980, one no longer need to ask if published, but only need to ask is it FIXED?

Fixed → Life + 70-years

SOMETHING TO THINK ABOUT:
Suppose in 1986 an author assigns rights to Paramount Studios in her short story.
Under § 203(a), author can terminate 35 years from date of assignment (not fixation).
Author has 5 years to effect termination (35 - 40 years)
Could give latest notice in year 2024 (2 years notice from 2026 (40-years)).
Illustrated above is termination of right to use original work and capacity to make further derivative works. Derivative works created before termination is not terminated. (Can exploit in any form but cannot redo).

After termination, derivative work's distribution rights remain with derivative work. Can't use underlying work any more (these rights terminated). Not going to let underlying author restrict derivative work's distribution. Allowed to use underlying work during notice period, up until date of termination. Incentive to make derivative works if underlying work still has value.

One can continue to manufacturer derivative works as long as it is not a new work. One can use anything that is created by termination, not necessarily marketed.
If 90% of work done by termination date, one is allowed to finish if what is left does not involve underlying work. Otherwise will

hold work hostage (great expense for negotiation and litigation) great incentive to finish work before termination date.
Termination only an issue if after 35 years.

SOMETHING TO THINK ABOUT:

Suppose a work was created in 1970 (fixed and published). When does it fall into public domain?

Automatic renewal for works created between 1964 and 1977 (does not matter if he forgets in 1998). Can save rights from going into public domain. If work pre-1964, and no renewal, falls into public domain.

An incentive in having author renew even though automatic renewal is to allow recovery of statutory damages.
Automatic renewal created for case where, for example, movie house cannot find author. But incentives created so movie house finds author. (Started to draft day after *Stewart v. Abend, supra*)

D. Termination

1. Termination of Transfers

Authors who assign their copyright interests to others should be able, after a reasonable time, to regain those interests, i.e., to "terminate" their transfers.

§ 203 applies to transfers made on or after January 1, 1978 and permits termination at a specified interval after the date of the grant.

§ 304(c) applies to works that were in their renewal term on January 1, 1978, and allows the author or her surviving family to terminate transfers made before that date, so as to recover the 19-year "bonus" period appended by the 1976 Act to the 1909 Act's 28-year renewal term.

If work is not in the public domain as of October 27, 1998, the Sonny Bono Copyright Term extension Act grants an additional 20 years of protection, thereby allowing a 39-year "bonus" period.

Termination Is Not Automatic: If the author or her family fails to take the necessary steps within the statutory time period, the transfer continues in accordance with the terms of the grant itself.

35 years following a grant, the author can go back to assignee and renegotiate.
Termination rights are INALIENABLE (cannot buy or sell termination rights).
This provision mirrors the 1909 Act, but avoids outcome of *Fred Fisher Music Co. v. Witmark & Sons, supra*.

2. Termination Under § 203

Termination of transfers under § 203 apply to grants made after 1977. Another way to state the same important point is this: when the copyright came into existence is irrelevant for determining whether § 203 applies. All that matters is the date of the transfer.

A provision of this sort is needed because of the unequal bargaining position of authors, resulting in part from the impossibility of determining a work's value until it has been exploited.

The termination of a transfer or license under § 203 would require the serving of an advance notice within specified time limits and under specified conditions. The scope of the right would extend not only to any "transfer of copyright ownership," as defined in § 101, but also to non-exclusive licenses.

a. Who can terminate a grant

Two issues emerged from the disputed over § 203 as to the persons empowered to terminate a grant:

- i. The specific classes of beneficiaries in the case of joint works; and
- ii. Whether anything less than unanimous consent of all those entitled to terminate should be required to make a termination effective.
  - a) In the case of joint works, majority action by those who signed the grant, or by their interests, would be required to terminate it.
  - b) There are three different situations in which the shares of joint authors, or of a dead author's widow or widower, children, and grandchildren, must be divided under the statute:

(1) The right to effect a termination;
(2) The ownership of the terminated rights; and
(3) The right to make further grants of reverted rights.

The respective shares of the authors, and of a dead author's widow or widower, children, and grandchildren, would be divided in exactly the same way in each of these situations. The term "widow," "widower," and "children" are defined in § 101 in an effort to avoid problems and uncertainties that have arisen under the present renewal section.

Consistent with the *per stirpes* principle, the interest of a dead child can be exercised only as a unit by majority action of his surviving children.

b. When a grant can be terminated

§ 203(a)(3) provides, as a general rule, that a grant may be terminated during the 5 years following the expiration of a period of 35 years from the execution of the grant.

As an exception to this basic 35-year rule, the bill also provides that "if the grant covers the right of publication of the work, the period begins at the end of 35 years from the date of publication of the work under the grant or at the end of 40 years from the date of execution of the grant, whichever term ends earlier."

The effective date of termination, which must be stated in the advance notice, is required to fall within the 5 years following the end of the applicable 35- or 40-year period, but the advance notice itself must be served earlier. Under § 203(a)(4)(A), the notice must be served "not less than two or more than ten years" before the effective date stated in it.

c. Effect of termination

§ 203(b) makes clear that, unless effectively terminated within the application 5-year period, all rights covered by an existing grant will continue unchanged.

Under the bill, termination means that ownership of the rights covered by the terminated grant reverts to everyone who owns termination interests on the date the notice of termination was served, whether they joined in signing the notice or not.

3. Termination under § 304(c)

§§ 304(a) and 304(b) add 39 years to the second or renewal term of protection for works copyrighted under the 1909 Act.

Through § 304(c), Congress created a "second chance" for such persons to benefit from the exploitation of commercially valuable works by permitting them to terminate, at least with respect to the 39-year extension, virtually all grants of renewal term interests. They receive an opportunity to regain their interest in the copyright during 39-year extension if they comply with certain carefully prescribed procedures.

If the work is not in the public domain as of October 27, 1978, the previous 19-year term is increased by 20 additional years under the Copyright Term Extension Act, thereby adding 39 years to the second or renewal term of protection.

The reach of § 304(c) is not limited to assignments of renewal expectancies; it also extends to a variety of other grants, including both exclusive and nonexclusive licenses.

In the case of either a first-term or renewal copyright already subsisting when the new statute becomes effective, any grant of rights covering the renewal copyright in the work, executed before the effective date, may be terminated under certain conditions and limitation.

The 5-year period during which termination could be made effective would start 56 years after copyright was originally secured.

4. Comparison of Termination Under §§ 203 and 304(c)

§ 203 deals with transfers of copyright, or interests in copyright, made on or after January 1, 1978, whether or not the copyright itself existed on that date.

§ 304(c) deals with assignment executed prior to the effective date of the new Act.

To understand §§ 203 and 304(c), think initially in terms of three categories: (1) copyright interests obtained and transferred after 1977; (2) copyrights obtained and assigned before 1978; and (3) copyrights obtained before 1978 but transferred in whole or in part after 1977.

5. Copyright Interests Obtained and Transferred After 1977

For copyrights arising after 1977, the new Act replaces its predecessor's complicate durational provisions with a life-plus-70-year term, at least in the typical case of a single creator not working for hire.

Under § 203, a transfer of a copyright or any interest therein, if made by the author, may be terminated by qualified person at any time within a 5-year "termination window" that typically opens 35 years after the transfer is executed.

Termination is effect by giving notice between 2 and 10 years prior to a date within the window.

6. Copyrights Obtained and Assigned Before 1978

For copyrights which came into being prior to 1978, the new Act leaves intact the durational period created under the 1909 Act, namely, a 28-year initial term with the possibility of a 28-year renewal term.

The 1976 Act extends this period, however, by tacking on an additional 39-year term. Thus, the focus of the § 304(c) termination right is not the first 56 years of a copyright obtained under the 1909 Act, but rather the 39 years added onto that period by the 1976 Act.

This previous 19 year term is increased to 39 years, unless the work entered the public domain prior to October 27, 1998.

Post-1977 Transfers of Pre-1978 Interests
The duration of copyrights obtained before 1978 is an augmented 1909 Act period (28+28+19 + 20 = 95 years), which approximated the period anticipated by the drafters of the 1976 Act under its life-plus-70-years term.

a. Transfers Covered
Unlike § 203, the language of § 304(c) specifically applies not only to grants made by the author, but also to those made by the author's widow, widower or children, and his/her next of kin.
§ 304(c) applies to grants covering the renewal term for copyrighted works.
§ 203 applies to any interest in copyright.

b. Person Qualified to Terminate

The persons who qualify to claim the extra 19 years granted by § 302(a) are set out in § 304(c)(1) and (2).

Under § 203(a)(1) and (2), a somewhat different list of persons is empowered to terminate grants made after 1977, although the provisions for the exercise of the right by a deceased author's survivors are identical.

c. Beginning of the Termination Window

Under § 304(c), reclamation of the extra 39 years granted to copyrights subsisting on the effective date of the new Act and subject to pre-1978 grants of the renewal term must be accomplished within a 5-year window beginning with the start of the 39-year period.

Under § 203, termination of a transfer made after 1977 must be done within the 5-year period beginning 35 years after the transfer.

d. Persons Who Make Further Grants

Under § 304(c)(6), each owner of a right which has reverted after termination of a transfer made by an

author's successor becomes a tenant in common entitled to deal separately with the right.
Under § 203(b), the situation is different. There is no tenancy in common. Instead, one the right in a post-1977 grant has been recovered, a majority of the owners thereof, voting in the statutorily prescribed fashion, may make further grants that bind the other owners as well.

7. Case Law

Burroughs v. Metro Goldyn-Mayer, Inc., 683 F.2d 610 (2d Cir. 1982)
This case involved an attempt to terminate a 1931 nonexclusive license to film rights with use of certain Tarzan characters. The nonexclusive license in question was given by a family-owned corporation, ERB, Inc., to MGM's predecessor in title. The author's heirs served notice of termination on the family-owned corporation, but not on MGM, in 1977, before the effective date of the 1976 Act. The plaintiffs contend that the Tarzan grant was effectively terminated and that a 1981 remake of Tarzan by MGM infringed their rights.

The District Court held that the character, Tarzan, was sufficiently delineated to be a copyrightable interest and as such could be terminated. The termination was ineffective, however, because it was premature (the Act was not yet in effect in 1977) and because it was served on the family-owned corporation (the original grantee) and not on the "current successor in title," MGM, as it should have been.

The Second Circuit affirmed the decision, but on different grounds, stating that the Copyright Office regulations require that notice of termination be accompanied by a short statement as to the grants covered. The plaintiffs, however, failed to list five titles of works in their notice of termination. The court concluded that this omission rendered the termination ineffective because the grant gave the right to use the Tarzan character for each of these titles. Thus, the grant remained intact because, to be effective, a notice of termination must clearly identify the grant to which the notice applies.

The case still leaves open the question of whether a notice of termination, to be effective, must be served on the grantee, the grantee's successor in title, or both. The statute provides that the notice must be served on the grantee or the grantee's successor in title. Judge Newman, in a concurring opinion suggested that notice must be served on MGM, because to allow the notice to be served on the family-owned corporation would be like allowing the heirs to serve notice on themselves.

One intermediate solution, supporting both the interest of the author and his grantee, would require the author to serve notice on the original grantee and his exclusive licensee, but not on nonexclusive licensees. Today, one should use a catch-all phrase such as "terminate all works, listed or not." Court saying if want to terminate, must be specific. Thus, it is not enough to terminate the original, must terminate everything.

Mills Music v. Albuquerque A.R.T. Co., 469 U.S. 153, 105 S. Ct. 638, 83 L. Ed.2d 556 (1985) (A derivative work prepared under a grant can continue to be used under its terms even after termination of the grant.

Section 304(c)(6)(A) Continued exploitation is limited to the specific derivative works and does not extend to preparation of other derivative works based on the copyright covered by the terminated grant.)

The issue was whether an author's termination of a music publisher's interest in a copyright also terminated the publisher's contractual right to share in the royalties from those whom he had sublicensed to make derivative works. Snyder (songwriter) assigned the renewal term to Mills Music. As owner of the renewal term to the song, Mills Music had sublicensed the song to more that 400 record companies, each of which had prepared separate derivative works and paid royalties. The author's family served on Mills Music notice of termination covering the 19-year extended renewal term and demanded that royalties revert to them.

The Supreme Court, reversing a decision in favor of Snyder, held that the use of the term "grant" three times in

§ 304(c)(6)(A) revealed a legislative intent to cover not only the original grant but he sublicense made under that grant as well. The Court acknowledged that the principal purpose of § 304 was to benefit authors, but recognized that his was not its sole rationale. Its other purpose was to enable continued public accessibility to derivative works after termination. The Court concluded that upholding the status quo did justice to both policies.
The dissent pointed out that a middleman assignee's right to receive continued royalties had nothing to do with continued public access to a work but would undermine the other policy of the 1976 Act, which is to benefit authors.

This is a hard case because statute does not give you the answer. What is termination? Under statute, grant is terminated (null and void). In general, copyright has ignored middlemen.

VI. PUBLICATION AND FORMALITIES

Before the 1976 Act took effect, unpublished works were protected by "common law" copyright in the states; published works were protected only by "statutory" copyright under federal law.

A. Publication

The dividing line between protection and nonprotection is creation (that is, the fixation of an original work).

1. Works fixed on or after January 1, 1978

Before March 1, 1989, publication without attending to the statutory formalities, particularity notice, still effects a forfeiture or abandonment.

After March 1, 1989, observation of notice formalities in connection with publication may enhance significantly the remedies available to a copyright owner bringing an action for infringement.

2. Works in their first (or original) term as of January 1, 1978

If the copyrights in such works arose prior to 1964 and were not properly renewed under old § 304(a), the works fell into the public domain.

If the copyrights were properly renewed, they acquired an additional 67 (47 + 20) years of protection.

3. Works in their second (or renewal) term as of January 1, 1978 (works published with notice prior to January 1, 1950)

Under the 1909 Act, the total of the original and renewal term would have been 56 years.
Under the 1976 Act, the total duration of such a copyright is 95 years, which the drafters of the Act thought approximated the "life plus 70" duration typical for works fixed after January 1, 1978.

Total term is now 95 years, unless work was in the public domain prior to October 27, 1998.

4. Works created but not federally copyrighted prior to January 1, 1978 (At least at one time had a common law copyright, but which had not obtained a statutory copyright prior to January 1, 1978.)

If the work had a subsisting state law copyright on that date, it was transmuted into a federal copyright by operation of § 303 of the 1976 Act.

If, however, the work had been the subject of a general publication without notice prior to January 1, 1978, it was divested of its common law copyright without being invested with statutory copyright, and has fallen into the public domain; it is not protected by any subsisting copyright and cannot be made the basis of an action for infringement.

5. Federal Preemption of Rights Equivalent to Copyright

Under § 301, a work would obtain statutory protection as soon as it is "created" or, as that term is defined in § 101, when it is "fixed in a copy or phonorecord for the first time."

Main arguments for a single Federal system:

i. Promote national uniformity.
ii. Help give a clear interpretation of "publication."
iii. § 301 will implement the "limited times" provision of the Constitution; and
iv. Need for effective international copyright relations.

B. Limited Publication versus General Publication

A limited publication is a non-divestive publication which communicates the contents of a work to a narrowly selected group for a limited purpose, without transferring the rights of diffusion, reproduction, distribution, or sale. A limited publication is one in which circulation of the work is restricted both as the person who receive it and the purpose for its distribution. Otherwise, it is a general publication.

Because it focuses on the copyright owner's purpose in publishing the work, the limited publication doctrine contradicts the general rule that a person's subjective intent is irrelevant in deciding whether a publication has taken place.

Estate of Martin Luther King, Jr. v. CBS, 194 F.3d 1211 (11th Cir. 1999) (King's estate sued CBS for copyright infringement for using 60% of King's "I Have a Dream" speech in a video-documentary. CBS maintained that King had delivered the speech into the public domain and refused to pay royalties to King's estate. The district court declared that King's speech was a general publication, thereby entering it into the public domain, and granted summary judgment for CBS. King's estate appealed.)

The court analyzed this case using the Copyright Act of 1909, instead of 1976, because King received his copyright for the speech in 1963.

Under the 1909 Act, state common law protection automatically began when the speech was created and continued until general publication. General publication occurred: (a) if the work was distributed to the public in a format allowing public control over the work or (b) presented to the public in a format which would allow unrestricted copying. "The case law indicates that distribution to the news media, as opposed to the general public, for the purpose of enabling the reporting of a contemporary newsworthy event, is only a limited publication." Therefore, despite the fact that King's speech had a large radio and television audience, it was distributed to news agencies as a limited publication.

C. What is Publication?

If been distributed, a general use is usually for money (meant to distribute) while a limited use (sent to mom) will not give effect to § 10 under the 1909 Act.

Under 1909 Act, § 10 deals with publication of work with notice.

Publication not requirement for 1976 Act.

Under the Copyright Act of 1976, "a public performance or display of a work does not of itself constitute publication."

§ 101 (definition of "publication").

Forfeiture typically occurs through publication without proper notice and is accomplished by operation of law.

Abandonment requires intent, usually evidenced by an overt act such as a statement appearing on copies of the work that anyone who wishes to reproduce, perform or display the work is free to do so.
The statutory definition of publication in § 101 of the 1976 Act says nothing about where the relevant "sale or other transfer of ownership, or . . . rental, lease or lending" must take place.

Academy of Motion Pictures Arts & Sciences v. Creative House Promotions, Inc., 944 F.2d 1446 (9th Cir. 1991)

The Academy had distributed 158 copies of its famed Oscar statuette to award winners between 1929 and 1941, without notice of copyright and without any express restriction on the recipient's right to sell or dispose of their Oscar. In 1941, the Academy registered their claim to copyright, and from that time, all Oscars have borne notice of copyright. In 1976, the defendant commissioned a trophy sculptor to create a sculpture strikingly similar to the Oscar, which it sold to various corporate buyers.

The district court ruled that the Oscar had entered the public domain in 1941, because the Academy's divestive and general publication, without notice, triggered the loss of copyright.

The Court of Appeals reversed because the Oscars were distributed to a select group of persons for a limited purpose. Although there was no express restrictions on the use or distribution of the Oscar before 1941, the Ninth Circuit held that such restrictions were implied (no one ever offered to sell Oscar; each Oscar personalized; Academy never gave the recipients the permission to sell, distribute, or make other copies of their Oscars).

Under the 1909 Act, if one does not conform with formalities (registration, notice before publication), then the work will go into the public domain.

Under 1976 Act, copyright begins with fixation (to get into public domain, need 70 years after life of author to pass.)
This case is fact bound. Thus, courts will decide on a case by case basis and will weigh factors in many different ways. The outcome is therefore unpredictable.

SOMETHING TO THINK ABOUT:

Suppose you write a short story and give to:

- 5 relatives to comment - This is a limited use.
- Your copyright class - This is a limited use.
- Your entire law school - This is a limited use.
- To the New York Times - This is a general use because you lost control over who gets it.

D. Notice

Under the 1909 Act, terms of copyright ran from the date of publication, so that notice had an obvious utility.

Under the 1976, most works are protected for fixed terms related to the length of their authors' lives, making calculation of the term on the basis of the date of the copyright notice impossible.

As of March 1, 1989, the use of copyright notice ceased to be mandatory under American law.

The U.S. Copyright Office has not spoken on the issue of whether work first published with notice before March 1, 1989, and reprinted after March 1, 1989 should bear the copyright notice.

Under the present law the copyright notice serves four principal functions:

i. It has the effect of placing in the public domain a substantial body of published material that no one is interested in copyrighting;
ii. It informs the public as to whether a particular work is copyrighted;

iii. It identifies the copyright owner; and
iv. It shows the date of publication.

§401(b) sets out the form of notice to appear on visually-perceptible copies ("Copyright," "Copr.," or "©"; the year of first publication; and the name of the copyright owner)
A minority of courts have allowed the use of "©" as a copyright symbol. This is because in computer programs (ASCII) there is no © symbol available. However, very few courts have allowed this symbol to protect the author's rights. In the case of ASCII it is recommended that the author use "copyright" or "Copr.".

§401(b)(2) - in the case of a derivative work or compilation, it is not necessary to list the date of publication of all preexisting material incorporated in the work.

§401 (b)(3) - Recognizable abbreviation or a generally known alternative designation may be used instead of the full name of the copyright owner.

§401(c) provides that the notice "shall be affixed to the copies in such manner and location as to give reasonable notice of the claim of copyright."
Example: © 1999 Law Rules Publishing Corporation

1. Notice on Phonorecords of Sound Recordings

In general, the form of the notice specified by § 402(b) consists of the symbol "P"; the year of first publication of the sound recording; and the name of the copyright owner or an admissible variant.

There are three reasons for prescribing use of the symbol "P" rather than "©":

i. Avoid confusion between copyright in the sound recording and in the musical or literary work embodied in it;

ii. Distinguishing between copyright claims in the sound recording and in the printed test or art work appearing on the record label, album cover, etc.; and
iii. Symbol "P" has been adopted as the international symbol for the protection of sound recordings.

2. Position of Notice

The notice should be placed on the copy or phonorecord in such a manner and location as to "glue reasonable notice of the claim of copyright." Notice on a phonorecord may be on a label or container as long as it gives reasonable notice.

3. Notice for Publications Incorporating United States Works

Requires that when the copies or phonorecords consist "preponderantly of one or more works of the United States Government," the copyright notice (if any) identify those parts of the work in which copyright is claimed.

Example: © 1999 Law Rules Publishing Corporation. Copyright claimed in Sections 2-5, exclusive of U.S. Government maps.

4. Notice for Contributions to Collective Works

Basic approach:

i. To permit but not require a separate contribution to bear its own notice;
ii. To make a single notice, covering the collective work as a whole, sufficient to satisfy the notice requirement for the separate contributions it contains, even if they have been previously published or their ownership is different; and
iii. To protect the interests of an innocent infringer of copyright in a contribution that does not bear its own notice, who has dealt in good faith with the person named in the notice covering the collective work as a whole.

§ 404(b) - A separate contribution that does not bear its own notice, and that is published in a collective work with a general notice containing the name of someone other than the copyright owner of the contribution, is treated as if it has been published with the wrong name in the notice.

5. Omission of Copyright Notice

Under the proposed law, a work published without any copyright notice will still be subject to statutory protection for at least 5 years, whether the omission was partial or total, unintentional or deliberate.

§ 405(a) provides that omission of notice, whether intentional or unintentional, does not invalidate the copyright:

i. If "no more than a relatively small number" or copies or phonorecords have been publicly distributed without notice; **or**

ii. If registration for the work has already been made, or is made within 5 years after the publication without notice, and a reasonable effort is made to add notice to copies or phonorecords publicly distributed in the United States after the omission is discovered. (This is unlike the 1909 Act, which didn't allow for curing of omissions of notice.)

Current notice requirements are unchanged for works first published before the effective date of the Act. These works will fall into the public domain if published without notice, and registration is not made before or within 5 years of publication.

6. Case Law

Hasbro Bradley, Inc. v. Sparkle Toys, Inc., 780 F.2d 189 (2d Cir. 1985) (The plaintiff, a toy manufacturer, brought an action to enjoin an admitted copyist from distributing its Transformer brand robot toys in the United States. The defendant claimed that copyright was forfeited by the Japanese company, the assignor to Hasbro and the originator of the toys, in deliberately omitting notice from 213,000 of the toys sold in Asia.)

The court held that the assignor's deliberate omission of notice was indeed discovered by the assignee who was then attempting to cure the omission.

In addition to registration, § 405(a)(2) requires that the copyright owner make a reasonable effort to add notice to all copies or phonorecords that are publicly distributed before March 1, 1989. By this provision, the copyright owner does not have to make a reasonable effort to add notice to copies already possessed by members of the public. On the other hand, the copyright owner has a clear duty to affix notice to copies still in his possession awaiting distribution. The reasonable effort requirement is a question of fact to be worked out under the circumstances of each case. The general rule is that a copyright owner who can establish impracticality is excused.

To protect economic and proprietary interests in this intellectual material, the notice requirement applied equally to works published abroad.

Although a showing of irreparable harm is normally required, courts have held that such harm may be presumed when the plaintiff makes out a prima facie case of infringement.

Whether Hasbro cured Takara's omission of notice is determined by looking at § 405(a)(2):

i. Register within 5 years after publication without notice.
ii. Reasonable effort is made to add notice to copies or phonorecords publicly distributed in the United States after the omission is discovered.

Berne Convention prohibits the imposition of formalities. A defendant cannot use the benefit of innocent infringement in mitigation of actual or statutory damages.

§ 401(c) states that one "shall be affixed to the copies in such manner and location as to give reasonable notice of the claim of copyright."

SOMETHING TO THINK ABOUT:

Where should you place the copyright notice on a:

- Poster: Should put © on front, not back.
- Prism art sold in frame: Okay to put © on frame ("container") otherwise would ruin artwork.
- Wood mobile: No copyright notice is needed because in industry under constructive notice.

Suppose you distributed 100,000 toys without ©. Six months later you discover that the copyright notice is missing. What do you do?

i. Register ©.
ii. Reasonable efforts to add © notice

Need to attach notice to products in warehouse and include on all new products.
Don't need to go into private homes.

What about products on store shelves?
Fight over what distribute to public means: On store shelves or in the hands of the public.
Courts determine "reasonable efforts" and "public" together.

VII. INFRINGEMENT ACTIONS

§ 501(a) identifies a copyright infringer as someone who "violates any of the exclusive rights of the copyright owner as provided by §§ 106 - 20" of the bill, or who imports copies or phonorecords in violation of § 602.

§ 501(b) enables the owner of a particular right to bring an infringement action in that owner's name alone, while at the same time insuring to the extent possible that the other owners whose rights may be affected are notified and given a chance to join the action.

A "beneficial owner" for this purpose would include, for example, an author who had parted with legal title to the copyright in exchange for percentage royalties based on sales or license fees.

§ 501(b) is intended to allow a court to permit or compel joinder of the owners of rights in works upon which a derivative work is based.

To be held a related or vicarious infringer in the case of performing rights, a defendant must either actively operate or supervise the operation of the place wherein the performances occur, or control the content of the infringing program, and expect commercial gain from the operation and either direct or indirect benefit from the infringing performance.

A. Jurisdiction

28 U.S.C. § 1338(a) gives federal courts exclusive jurisdiction for action arising under the Copyright Act.

To determine that an action arises under the 1976 Copyright Act requires distinguishing between an action based primarily on a right conferred by the 1976 Copyright Act, and an action incidentally involving issues of copyright law.

A suit for statutory copyright infringement is the classic example of an action expressly conferred by copyright, where federal jurisdiction is exclusive.

By comparison, an action brought to enforce an assignment of copyright is essentially an action under contract law. Here, the state court jurisdiction would be exclusive, even though the state court may have to interpret aspects of copyright law to determine whether to enforce the assignment. Similarly, an action brought to enforce royalties under a licensing agreement would lie essentially in the domain of state law, as would a will conveying a copyright and an action to foreclose a statutory copyright mortgage.

Even where the action does not involve statutory copyright infringement, exclusive jurisdiction will be conferred if the complaint necessitates construction or application of provisions of the 1976 Copyright Act.

Often a complaint will include both federal as well as non-federal claims. Under 28 U.S.C. § 1338(a), the federal court must determine whether it has jurisdiction to decide the case under the copyright laws. Under 28 U.S.C. § 1338(b), a district court has the power to decide the nonfederal claim if three jurisdictional requirements are met:

i. The basis of the nonfederal claim must be "unfair competition," and the federal claim to which it is attached must be both;
ii. Substantial; and
iii. Related.

As for the requirement that the state claim constitute "unfair competition," the courts have broadly construed them to include claims of passing off, misappropriation, misrepresentation, conversion, trade secret misappropriation, and breach of contract.

As for the "substantiality" of the claim, the courts will deny jurisdiction over the state cause of action if the federal claim is denied on a pretrial motion.

Two views exist on the meaning of "related" for the purpose of pendent jurisdiction.

i. The more restrictive view holds that the two claims are related only if they rest on substantially identical facts.
ii. The more liberal view, which appears to be the current trend, holds that the two claims are related if they have the same "factual nucleus,"

even though they might not derive from identical facts.

T.B. Harms Co. v. Eliscu, 339 F.2d 823 (2d Cir. 1964)
This case is about "arising under" jurisdiction of 28 U.S.C. § 1338. There is no federal jurisdiction if only arguing over state claim. One needs "arising under" jurisdiction to get into federal court.
If there is a contract question (interpretation), the cause of action is out of federal court's jurisdiction. However, if there is a federal statutory question, then federal court can decide.
The parties are not fighting about the length of the renewal, the procedure of the renewal, or whether the widow has a claim, but rather the contract they entered into. Thus, state law applies and case should be heard in state court. Attorney tried to get into federal court by making question look like a federal question.

Once you get into federal court under either federal question or diversity jurisdiction, you can bring in other non-federal claims provided both claims are arise out of the same transaction or occurrence.

SOMETHING TO THINK ABOUT:

Suppose you make an oral agreement with a law school's law review to publish an article by May 1995. You decide in May 1996 to publish your own book which includes a chapter of the article you submitted to the law review to publish. Your book including the article chapter is published in May 1997. Can the law review sue you? What is the effect of oral contract?

Generally, law review would not have exclusive license, but rather would only have a non-exclusive license. Therefore, the cause of action would be interpreted under state contract law. (But may have to look at contract with particular law school's law review to check to see what type of license was assigned.)

One should draft the pleadings in a way to determine jurisdiction, either federal or state. (*See Schoenberg v. Shapolsky Publishers, Inc.* (1992))

Friedman, Eisensteink, Raemer & Schwartz v. Afterman, 599 F. Supp 902 (N.D. Ill. 1984)

Plaintiff published "Practitioners Technical Bulletin;" Defendant, who formerly worked for plaintiff, published "Accounting & Auditing Update Services;" Defendant breached covenant of non-competition.
The issue in the case is whether the plaintiff's state law claims and the copyright claim are derived from a common nucleus of operative facts. The federal law issue is whether under the work-for-hire doctrine the defendant was an employee at the time of he wrote the copyrighted material. If he was, then the plaintiff owns the work. The state law issue is whether the defendant breached his covenant not to compete.

The case was properly decided in federal court because both issues derive from a common nucleus of operative facts. Thus, under the theory of pendent claim jurisdiction if jurisdiction lies in federal court, non-federal issues as well as federal claims may be heard in federal court.

1. Procedure and Remedies §§ 500's

Possible Remedies

i. Injunctions
ii. Damages
iii. Profits
iv. Statutory damages
v. Attorney's fees

Swarovski America Ltd. v. Silver Deer Ltd., 537 F. Supp 1201 (D. Colo. 1982) (Plaintiff alleges that the defendants infringed the plaintiff's copyright in certain crystal figurines by authorizing their manufacture and by distributing them to the public.)

§ 205 of the Copyright Act of 1976 allows recordation in the Copyright Office of all documents of copyright ownership whether assignment, exclusive licenses, or nonexclusive licenses. To fully enjoy the benefits of the 1976 Act, an owner of a copyright interest should accompany the recordation with a registration of the underlying work.
An owner of an exclusive license to perform a copyrighted work cannot defend his rights in a court of law without recording his exclusive license in the Copyright Office.
For causes of action arising on or after March 1, 1989, recordation as a prerequisite to bringing a copyright

infringement suit is no longer required. However, one should still record because:

i. Recordation specifically identifying the work will give notice to the world of the terms set forth in the document; and
ii. Recordation establishes priority of ownership between conflicting transfers of copyright as well as conflicts between a transfer and a nonexclusive license.

The author is not required to be joined because it may be hard to join everyone in the case. The author would later be estopped from suing because of *res judicata*. Thus, under § 501(b) this is permissive joinder not compulsive.
The statute says that non-exclusive licensee may not sue because of unjust enrichment, *res judicata*, and it would discourage oral contracts. Thus, there is no federal remedy, but there might be a state remedy.
If have exclusive license, you may sue in federal court.

Cortner v. Israel, 732 F.2d 267 (2d Cir. 1984) (1984) Plaintiff composed music "ABC, Monday Night Football" theme. ABC and plaintiff were the copyright owners. They had a contract for royalties; ABC commissioned defendant to write a new, similar theme song and ABC held the copyright under the work-made-for-hire doctrine. Plaintiff sued defendant for copyright infringement.

Court held that it lacks diversity jurisdiction and affirmed the district court's decision.
District Court affirmed.

§ 501(b) states that the legal or beneficial owner of a copyright has an exclusive right. Beneficial owner not defined in § 101, but from legislative history it is an author who had parted with legal title to the © in exchange for % royalties based on sales or license fees.
Therefore, appellants have standing of infringement under either act as beneficial owner. ABC is not liable because it is the copyright owner and Israel and Score are not liable because they were commissioned by the copyright right owner to create a work-made-for-hire.

Demetriades v. Kaufmann, 690 F. Supp 289 (S.D.N.Y. 1988)
The court concluded that infringement could be found if they had copied in whole or in part the floor plans from the brochures in making their own architectural plans, even if these same plans would give the copyright owner no claim over the features they detail. However, these limitations on copyright for architecture have been removed by the 1990 amendments.
The Second Circuit has noted that vicarious liability is "when the right and ability to supervise [the infringer] coalesce (unites) with an obvious and direct financial interest in the exploitation of copyrighted materials," a third party may be held liable for the direct infringement by another. However, the doctrine of "vicarious liability" is inapplicable in this case.

2. Burden of Proof

The plaintiff in a copyright action is responsible for proving:

i. His or her ownership of the pertinent exclusive right(s) in the accusing work; and
ii. A *prima facie* case of infringement of the right(s) in suit by the defendant.

Once a *prima facie* case has been established by the plaintiff, the defendant bears the burden of rebutting that case, including any of the limitations found in §§ 107-20, which act as affirmative defenses.

As to ownership, the principal matters to be proved include: the copyrightability of the work; its authorship by the plaintiff; the plaintiff's citizenship status; compliance with any statutory formalities; and the basis of the plaintiff's claim to ownership if he or she obtained title to the right in suit subsequent to registration of the copyright.

While the *prima facie* presumption of ownership, once established by the plaintiff, is rebuttable, "defendant must meet a very high burden of proof to overcome that presumption.

B. Substantive Aspects

Proof of infringement has two components:

i. The plaintiff must demonstrate that the defendant did, in fact, copy material from the copyrighted work.
ii. The plaintiff must show that the defendant's copying constitutes an improper appropriation.

"Copying" almost always is proved by indirect i.e., circumstantial evidence of the defendant's infringing activity, simply because direct evidence is not available. Accordingly, the courts are forced to presume copying upon proof that the defendant had "access" to the copyrighted work, usually coupled with proof of some degree of similarity between that work and the alleged infringing work.

"Improper appropriation" is a separate matter. Even if the defendant cannot rebut the plaintiff's case on copying, he or she still may escape liability if the plaintiff fails to show that the taking was impermissible as to both kind and amount.

i. The plaintiff must demonstrate that what the defendant appropriated from the copyrighted work was protected expression.
ii. The plaintiff must show that the intended audiences for the two works will find "substantial similarity" between the defendant's work and the plaintiff's protected expression.

In short, if both copying and improper appropriation are demonstrated, the plaintiff has made out a *prima facie* case.

1. Copying

Bright Tunes Music Corp. v. Harrisongs Music, Ltd., 420 F.Supp 177 (S.D.N.Y. 1976)
Access has been inferred where the work was in possession of a third party which had done business with both plaintiff and defendant, or where the work was available to employees in defendant corporation's files. Alternatively, evidence of access was insufficient to support a claim for infringement where nothing more could be shown other than the work was available in defendant's city of residence.
In this case, access to a famous, widely-disseminated work may also be inferred where facts suggest that defendant had a reasonable opportunity to view or copy it.

The court found that defendant had access to the copyrighted work because of its popularity as a hit in the United States and abroad. And even though defendant may have unintentionally copied it through subconscious processes, unintentional copying does not constitute a defense against an action for copyright infringement.

To prove access, plaintiff must show that defendant had a reasonable opportunity to view or copy the work. Generally, the evidence must be sufficient for the trier of fact to infer a reasonable probability of access. On the other hand, a mere possibility of access, based on conjecture or speculation, is not enough to make the circumstantial case.

Strikingly Similar: When two works are so strikingly similar that independent creation is not reasonably possible. To infer access in this situation, plaintiff must show similarities that could only be explained by copying rather than by coincidence, independent creation, or use of a prior common source. The nature of the copyrighted work is the essential factor in making the circumstantial case in this situation.

Selle v. Gibb, 741 F.2d 896 (7th Cir. 1984)
The question involved in this case was whether the Bee Gee's international hit song "How Deep Is Your Love" was so strikingly similar to defendant's prior song that proof of access could be inferred.
The court held that even strikingly similarity is not enough to infer access unless there is some evidence making it reasonably possible that plaintiff's work was available to the infringer. Some courts feel that if two works are strikingly similar, then the subsequent author must have had access and will therefore find infringement.
Here the reasonable possibility does not exist. The Bee Gee's song was written in France, while the plaintiff's song was limited to play in the Chicago area. Moreover, the songs did not involve the kind of striking similarity sufficient to overcome the need to show reasonable opportunity to copy.

When the works are trite or commonplace and resemble available public sources, the fact that they are similar does not support the inference that the work was copied, and other proof of access showing a reasonable opportunity to view the work will be required.

SOMETHING TO THINK ABOUT:
Why able to get statutory damages when only able to prove substantial similarity?
Don't have right to statutory damages.
Discretion only goes to the amount of damages. Thus, while an innocent infringer should pay nothing, the minimum is $500.
As a matter of fact, Judge has equitable power to award remedies.

The following sections of the statute support why substantial similarity is enough to award damages:
§ 101 ('derivative work'), § 103(b), § 106(2), § 107(3), § 108(e).
If one limits copyright infringement to literal copying, someone can go ahead and steal your market.
Type of copying will influence judge when determining damages. What is substantial? How little copying is enough?

2. Improper Appropriation

Subtractive Approach to Substantial Similarity:
After the unprotected elements are "subtracted," so to speak, the finder-of-fact proceeds to ask whether there are significant similarities between what remains of the allegedly infringed work, on the one hand, and the various components and characteristics of the allegedly infringing work, on the other.

Three Boys Music Corp. v. Bolton, 212 F.3d 477 (9th Cir. 2000) (The Isley Brothers, a popular 60's group, created and copyrighted the song "Love is a Wonderful Thing." In early 1990, Michael Bolton released a song "Love is a Wonderful Thing." The Isley Brothers sued Bolton for copyright infringement. The district court found that the Bolton song was substantially similar to the 1966 Isley release and that Bolton had subconsciously copied the song. Bolton appealed.)

Especially in music cases, the proof of copyright infringement is highly circumstantial. To prove copyright infringement, the plaintiff must prove ownership of a valid copyright and infringement (e.g., that the defendant copied protected elements of the plaintiff's work), which is proven by access and substantial similarity. The court affirmed the jury's holding, finding that despite this being a "weak case of access and a circumstantial case of substantial similarity," the verdict should not be second-guessed because it is supported by substantial evidence. Although the inverse ratio rule requires a lesser showing of substantial similarity if there is a stronger proof of access or vice versa, it does not inversely mean that a weak showing of access requires a stronger showing of substantial similarity.

Totality Approach. Under this "total concept and feel" approach, the ultimate role of the finder-of-fact is to determine whether the accused and complaining works would have the same appeal to the relevant audience for the works.

***Nichols v. Universal Pictures Corp.*,** 45 F.2d 229 (1930)
Judge Learned Hand made a famous attempt to draw the line between taking idea and taking expression.
Plaintiff-author of the play "Abie's Irish" Rose sued defendant for its motion picture "The Cohens and the Kelleys". The issue was whether the play and the movie were substantially similar, given the obvious similarity of the storylines of the two shows.
The court concluded that "[T]he only matter common to the two is a quarrel between a Jewish and an Irish father, the marriage of their children, the birth of grandchildren and a reconciliation.

The abstractions test (formulated by, Judge Learned Hand) provides insight into how to separate copyrightable expression from non-infringing public domain ideas to determine substantial similarity. The test may be viewed as a continuum with pure idea at one end and pure expression at the other. As the idea travels along continuum (uninterrupted), it gathers concrete details and becomes more complex. No longer a vague set of generalities, it

cannot be summed up in a few words. A taking at this point is a taking of the author's expression.
Although the abstractions test is a useful conceptualization of the problem, it does not clearly indicate where on the continuum an undue amount of plaintiff's expression has been taken. Perhaps all that can be said is that there comes a point where defendant's use of the general theme combines with similarities in details, scenes, sequence of events, characterization, and interplay of characters to constitute infringement.

SOMETHING TO THINK ABOUT:
Suppose every year a family goes on vacation to Jackson Hole, Wyoming. The family is made up of some very unique characters. The family gets into a heated discussion about whether one member of the family should be a single parent. One night, two different members of the family writer their version of the story and produce plays on Broadway. Who would prevail?
How was the expression similar? Distinction from *Nichols* not drawing from general character types.
Was there copying? Was there access? (actual or circumstantial evidence: capacity of access.

Suppose one stole papers from the other and then wrote story based on this. Who should prevail?
Court must decide who did it first, who had access. If expression is the same, then there was likely to be copy. However, be careful because based on factual event.

***Scenes a fair*:** Scene must be essential to play and commonly associated. Exclude stock characters and certain character relationships. One can get copyright protection for arrangement, which is similar to the compilation statute.
Each circuit have general trend (analytic or "look and feel" approach") (Supreme Court never said either one must be used.)
One can overcome the presumption of access by disproving access.

Peter Pan Fabrics, Inc. v. Martin Weiner Corp., 274 F.2d 487 (2d Cir. 1960)
Graphic designs for textiles were also included within copyrightable subject matter of pictorial, graphic, and sculptural works (implied).
A flexible approach was taken to notice of copyright placed on the selvage of a fabric design which would either be cut off from the fabric or rendered undetectable on a dress.

Commercial impairment test (adopted by Judge Learned Hand) in which, at least in the case of deliberate copyist, the defendant has the burden to show that notice could have been embodied in the design without impairing it market value.

SOMETHING TO THINK ABOUT:
Suppose you create a magic card game, but they do not look like usual card. Someone else plays game by using an ordinary deck. Is there © infringement?

NO - One cannot copyright the game idea, but perhaps the "look and feel" of the design of the cards.

COPYING = ACCESS + PROBATIVE (Substantial) SIMILARITY

COPYRIGHT = COPYING & INFRINGEMENT MISAPPROPRIATION

Laureyssens v. Idea Group, Inc., 964 F.2d 131 (2d Cir. 1992)
(Two foam rubber puzzles were created that looked similar.)
What test do you apply (standard) to determine if substantial similarity? lay observer.
Court concluded that the puzzles were similar. The copyright was for the pieces, not for puzzle as a whole. But nothing in statute tells you to look at pieces themselves instead of overall effect.
The idea of a flat-to-cube puzzle is not copyrightable because one cannot protect this idea. Can protect expression of idea (pieces), but may not protect structure together.
If the court used the total concept and feel test, it would have come out with a different result.

The court used analytical test. (Abstraction/Filtration)

Sliding Scale in Copying: The more two works look strikingly similar than the courts will assume access. This establishes a lower burden of access (this depends on circuit).

If two works are probatively similarity, then the court must prove access (either direct or indirect).

COPYRIGHT INFRINGEMENT = COPYING + UNLAWFUL APPROPRIATION

Coping is the threshold issue.

Unlawful appropriation takes into consideration what test to use (common lay observer or expert).

Lay-observer test can be used for analytical test or total concept test.

One will be told what test to apply and what standard to use. Music industry have been good about using expert standard (but still can be applied to either test). See both types of standards and observers in copying and unlawful appropriation (more helpful in unlawful appropriation).

Jury instructions are usually challenged, law unclear in this area. Likely to get copyright infringement when have some similarity and ask lay observer to compare total-concept. (Judge may award smaller damages though).

Normally, Judge decides copying, not jury. Some works get opinion letter from © office, can block registration. Go to court.

3. Computer Programs

Under § 101, a computer program is "a set of statements or instructions to be used directly or indirectly in a computer in order to bring about a certain result".

a. Similarity between computer programs:
Computer program may be considered a literary work under
§ 102(a)(1), but it does not appear in § 117. However, the term "include" is illustrative and not limitative.

If a computer program is considered a procedure, process, system, then it is not copyrightable.

Baker v. Selden , 101 U.S. 99, 11 Otto 99, 25 Led. 841 (1880) is the closed case to computer program. Thus, absent merger problem, could have ©.

The test used depends on the circuit:

Second Circuit in *Altai* used the total concept or analytical approach.

Third Circuit in *Whalen* looked at the structure, sequence, organize to determine copying.

Now that computer programs are copyrightable subject matter and are protected against verbatim copying, the difficult question is to what extent programs are protected against nonliteral copying. The question is whether copyright protection will extend beyond the written code itself to the structure of the program and its user interface.

To determine how far computer programs should be protected against nonliteral copying should ultimately depend on whether the particular approach encourages the optimal production and dissemination of computer programs. Inadequate protection will undermine the incentive to create computer programs, whereas too much protection will unduly impede their dissemination and deprive creators of basic material on which they build their own works.

Computer Associates International, Inc., v. Atlai, Inc., 982 F.2d 963 (2d Cir. 1992)

Both plaintiff and defendant marketed a computer program that performed similar functions on IBM mainframe computers. Although the defendant's first version of the program had directly used significant parts of the code structure, the second version contained no program code in common with the plaintiff's software. The defendant conceded liability for copyright infringement for the first version of the program while denying that the second version infringed the plaintiff's copyright. The similarity between the programs, however, raised the question of how far copyright should go to protect the nonliteral elements of a program.

b. Analysis

The court developed *three stages of analysis*: abstraction, filtration, comparison:

i. ***Abstraction***: One must abstract the program into various layers of generality. Here, in a manner similar to reverse engineering, a court should dissect the copyrighted program's structure and isolate each level of abstraction in it.

ii. ***Filtration***: The merger doctrine can be used to filter out those elements of the program dictated by efficiency or by factors external to the program itself, e.g., mechanical specification, compatibility requirements or those taken from the public domain.

iii. ***Comparison***: Compare the remaining elements with the corresponding elements of defendant's work.

The court agreed with the district court that the program contained protectable elements similar to plaintiff's program. These similarities, however, were not sufficiently material to the overall program to uphold a finding of infringement.
This holding clearly narrows the scope of protection for nonliteral components of computer program.

SOMETHING TO THINK ABOUT:
Just because a computer program accomplishes certain ends does not necessarily preclude it from copyright protection. Look to the language in § 101.

Separate expression from function.
Left with expression.

Language not protected because they are rules or processes (not original expression).
Compiler may be protected, but will have hard time.
Grammar not protected.

Idea/expression dichotomy is not a bright line test. Program protected if original and fixed (originality is taken from universe of possibilities).

3 PART TEST FOR UNLAWFUL APPROPRIATION:

Abstraction: Expression can turn into idea the more vague it is:

i. ***Conceptual separation test*** does expression embody an idea that may appear in a different expression; Stock and trade elements are segments that are used segment over and over again, and therefore are not copyrightable. Computer programs get thin protection because they use a lot of stock and trade elements. Repetition turns expression into idea; being driven to patent law standard.

ii. ***Filtration***: Go through pieces and see what is scope of plaintiff's copyright. Unlawful appropriation standard is used and test is similar to analytical test. Don't protect the elements that are necessary to run program.

iii. ***Comparison:*** Compare the remaining elements with the corresponding elements in defendant's work.

Determine if NO INFRINGEMENT between non-literal elements (beyond scope of object code). There was a lot less protection after *Computer Assocs.* than if court looked at the totality parts. (Damages probably less).

SOMETHING TO THINK ABOUT:

The abstraction - filtration - comparison test was originally designed for written or literary works. Now, in the computer age, courts are struggling to adopt this same test to computer programs.

C. Damages

1. Injunctive Relief

Under U.S.C. § 502, a court can grant temporary and permanent injunctions.

2. **Infringer Liability:** Under 17 U.S.C. § 504, an infringer of copyright is liable for either:
   i. the copyright owner's actual damages and any additional profits of the infringer; or
   ii. statutory damages.

Thus, if the copyright owner (or Plaintiff(s)) wants to seek actual damages and profits under 504(b), he/she is entitled to recover actual damages suffered as a result of the infringement (lost profits) and any profits of the infringer attributed to the infringement that were not taken into account in computing the actual damages. In establishing the infringer's profits, the copyright owner is only required to prove the infinger's gross revenue. After this is established, the burden shifts to the infringer to show what portion of total profits is attributable to deductible expenses, if any, and any non-infringing elements.

3. Monetary Relief -- Statutory Damages

Pursuant to § 504(c), the copyright owner may elect at any time before final judgment is rendered to recover in lieu of actual damages and profits an award of statutory damages for all infringements involved in the action with respect to any one work for which any one infringer is liable. Thus, under the current law, a copyright owner may elect to recover "a sum of not less than $500 or more than $20,000 as the court considers just" for each work that is infringed (rather than the number of infringements, as was the case under the 1909 Act). Although the term "work" is not defined in the statute, "all parts of a compilation or derivative work constitute one work."

These monetary limits imposed for statutory damages under §504(c)(1) have two exceptions under §504(c)(2):

i. **Willful infringement** - the court has discretion to increase the maximum award of damages to $100,000.

ii. **Innocent infringement** - the court has discretion to decrease the minimum award of damages to $200.

4. Cost and Attorney's Fees

§ 505 gives the court discretion to award the prevailing party of an action recovery of its full costs and/or attorney's fees.

5. Prerequisite for Statutory Damages and Attorney's Fees

§ 412 states that the election of statutory damages or recovery of attorney's fees is not available if:

i. the copyright infringement of an unpublished work began before the effective date of its registration; or
ii. the copyright infringement began after first publication of the work and before the effective date of its registration, unless the registration is made 3 months of the first publication of the work.

VIII. FAIR USE

Fair use is an affirmative defense that allows someone to lawfully copy another usually for educational purposes, reviews, comments, criticisms, etc.

Fair use finds its way in through legal misappropriation. Fair use is a defense to © infringement.
Every fair use case assumes copying.

To determine whether the use was a "fair use," the court looks at:

i. Purpose or character of the use;
ii. Nature of the copyrighted work;
iii. Amount and substantial portion of the underlying work that was used in relation to the copyrighted work as a whole; and
iv. Effect of the use upon the potential market.

The determination of fair use is extremely fact specific and there is no bright line test.

Sony Computer Entertainment v. Connectix, 203 F.3d 596 (9th Cir. 2000) (Connectix developed a video game system known as Virtual Game Station for personal computers, which is capable of using the Sony products that are designed for the Sony PlayStation. While developing the software, Connectix reverse engineered the Sony BIOS system. The district court granted Sony a preliminary injunction and Connectix appealed.)

The appellate court reversed the district court and determined that Connectix reverse engineering constituted fair use. The appellate court pointed out that software engineers often had to reverse engineer products to access functional elements. Such reverse engineering might necessitate copying the copyrighted program into a computer's RAM. In concluding that the Connectix acts of reverse engineering were a fair use as a matter of law, the court analyzed and weighed the four statutory factors of the fair use doctrine:

i. *Purpose and Character* – Connectix's Virtual Game Station was "modestly transformative," as it dealt with a new platform, the personal computer. When this was weighed against the other factors, including commercialism, Connectix's commercial use was only "indirect or derivative. Thus, this factor favored Connectix.

ii. *Nature of Use* – Connectix needed to copy the protected elements of the Sony BIOS system to access the non-protected elements. When such copying is "necessary," it constitutes fair use.

iii. *Amount and Substantial Portion of Underlying Work* – Connectix disassembled and made numerous copies of the Sony BIOS system. While this factor favors Sony, the court pointed out that when none of the intermediate work is incorporated into the final product, this factor carries "very little weight."

iv. *Effect on the Potential Market* – Connectix Virtual Game Station was a "legitimate" competitor with the Sony PlayStation. While Sony may suffer economic losses, copyright did not extend monopolistic protection to all platforms that play Sony games and devices.

SOMETHING TO THINK ABOUT:

Suppose a professor copies and distributes a newspaper article to class. Can the newspaper sue the professor for copying?
NO - Newspaper cannot sue because the use was for educational purposes.

Can professor copy a textbook?
NO - This would constitute a substantial portion under § 107(3).

Guidelines never enacted because publishers couldn't come to agreement. Need guidelines so teachers may decide what to use or not copy.
Intent of § 107 was to codification of existing common law principles.

Suppose author writes a letter and you write in newspaper "LOOK AT THIS (his entire letter)." Can author sue for infringement?
YES - He can sue for infringement and win because you used the entire thing (contributory negligence with newspaper).

§ 107(4): Effect on market for the work: letter of his for legal issues. MAYBE NOT MARKET.

§ 107(3): Amount and substantiality of portion (in trouble if take heart of the work).

Suppose author sends you outline of article.
This may hurt § 107(4) because article not published yet, but ideas out there.
§ 107(1): Purpose and character of the use.
§ 107(2): Nature of the copyrighted work.

The fact that work unpublished shall not itself bar a finding of fair use; unpublished works traditional reduce more protection because right of privacy (didn't intent to share).

Sony Corp. of America v. Universal City Studios, Inc., 464 U.S. 417, 104 S .Ct. 774, 748 L. Ed.2d 574 (1984) (People using betamax to tape TV and use TIME-SHIFTING. Universal sued Sony because deep pocket furnished people with device to copy.) Time shifting important because people not able to watch show during original time slot. They just watch and erase it when it is over. They do not tape in order to create a library of tapes.
Court said non-commercial use because the use was a private in the home and the people were not using it for resale. If this is infringement, then police would have to go into private homes to determine if illegal use. This constitutes an illegal search and seizure.

Europe has addressed this issue by charging a fee on all blank tapes, which is similar in concept to a copyright royalty.

IX. THE INTERNET AND CYBERLAW

A. Introduction

While the Internet has raised many challenging copyright issues, the most important rules to remember are the basic doctrines of copyright law.

After studying the preceding chapters, you should have a good idea of what constitutes a copyright and how it can be infringed. The intricacies of Internet copyright law arise from tensions in three areas:

1. New technologies and the degree of copyright protection (i.e., hyperlinking)
2. New uses of traditionally copyrighted materials (i.e., music, books)
3. New enforcement issues in copyright law (i.e., chat room owner liability)

To the layperson these cyberspace tensions seem new, but keeping copyright law abreast of new technologies is the perennial objective of copyright law.

1. New technologies

New technologies that are protected include:

a. Web sites including text and pictures
b. Software source/object codes
c. Internet products

Although protecting these new technologies may seem intuitive (i.e., a web page is similar to an audiovisual work), as the Internet evolves, new issues regarding these technologies arise.

One of the more recent technology cases involves hyperlinking, which allows a user browsing one web site to be transferred directly to a web page within another web site.

Ticketmaster Corp. v. Tickets.com Inc., 54 U.S.P.Q.2d 1344 (C.D. Cal. 2000) (Both Ticketmaster and Tickets.com provide information on events and ticket sales online. Ticketmaster sued Tickets.com for copyright infringement, basing its complaint on: (a) Tickets.com copied

Ticketmaster web pages to the Tickets.com web site to gather event information such as event, place, date, time, and price of ticket; (b) the factual information was then used on the Tickets.com web pages in a different format; and (c) Tickets.com also provided hyperlinks to the Ticketmaster web site but bypassed the Ticketmaster homepage.)

The court dismissed points (b) and (c), finding that neither the use of the factual information from another's web page nor hyperlinking to another's web page constitutes copyright infringement. The court, however, did not dismiss point (a) because it was based on actual copying of the web page.

2. New uses of traditionally copyrighted materials

Some web sites and service providers may be passive in contributing to copyright infringement, as they merely provide the medium or gateway for sharing and distributing copyrighted material. If these web sites and service providers are held liable for the copyright infringement of third parties, however, many people worry that the Internet will be stunted. Since the copyrighted works posted on these web sites still need to be protected, the courts are beginning to distinguish these cases and discuss the policies behind them.

National Basketball Association v. Motorola, 105 F.3d 841 (2nd Cir. 1997) (Motorola developed the SportsTrax pager, which delivered real-time information on NBA games including score, possession, and time. Reporters provide the SportsTrax pager information by entering data into a personal computer while watching/listening to the broadcast. This data is subsequently transmitted to the Sports Team Analysis and Tracking Systems' (STATS) "host computer," and then retransmitted in a standard format to the pager. NBA brought several charges including copyright infringement. The district court granted a permanent injunction and Motorola appealed.)

In vacating the permanent injunction, the court first considered whether the games themselves are copyrightable. Since the underlying basketball games do not fall within any of the enumerated categories of "works of authorship" covered by § 102(a), the court found these athletic events are not copyrightable. The court next considered whether SportsTrax infringed on the copyrighted broadcasts of the game. Pointing out that SportsTrax and the America Online web site only used the facts from the broadcasts, the court found that this does not constitute copyright infringement. Turning to the crux of the dispute, the court found that a narrow state law "hot-news" misappropriation claim based on *International News Service v. Associated Press* could survive preemption by the federal Copyright Act. In evaluating a "hot-news" misappropriation claim, the following factors are considered:

i. Cost to plaintiff to gather information
ii. Time-sensitivity of information
iii. Whether defendant's use constitutes "free riding" on plaintiff's efforts
iv. Whether competition between plaintiff and defendant is direct
v. If there were free riding, would the amount of individuals free-riding constitute a disincentive to continued service?

However, since each party is bearing its own costs in gathering the information and the NBA has not shown any damages based on "free-riding" by Motorola, the NBA's claim for misappropriation is dismissed as well.

UMG Recordings, Inc. v. MP3.com, Inc., 92 F. Supp.2d 349 (S.D.N.Y. 2000) (MP3 technology enables users to store music from a CD into a computer medium. MP3.com bought about 45,000 CDs, copied the songs contained on the CDs, and stored them as MP3 files. MP3.com then provided a service entitled "My.MP3.com," which enables users to listen to these MP3 files through the Internet. After initially demonstrating that a user owned a given CD, which can be done by placing it within their hard drive or buying it through one of MP3's preferred sites, the user could listen to the MP3 file through the internet anywhere. Plaintiffs' sued for copyright infringement.)

The court entered partial summary judgment for the plaintiffs holding MP3.com liable for copyright infringement. In rejecting MP3.com's fair use defense, the court stated that even if the user owned the CD at the time of initial subscription, the user was listening to an unauthorized copy of the CD supplied by MP3.com. The court found that MP3.com's purpose and character of use of My.MP3.com was commercial in nature (attract large subscription base to draw advertising), the files supplied by MP3.com were exact copies of the entire copyrighted works, and MP3.com was simply retransmitting the copyrighted work in a different medium.

A & M Records v. Napster, Inc., 2001 U.S. App. Lexis 5446 (9th Cir. 2001) (Through a peer-to-peer file sharing process, Napster allows or facilitates its users to share, copy, and exchange MP3 files for free through the internet. Plaintiff brought charges of contributory and vicarious copyright infringement against Napster. In defending its case, Napster argued that as an internet service provider, its web site was within the safe harbor provisions of the DCMA (see below). The district court ruled that Napster system did not fall within the safe harbor provision. Napster might assist users in sharing, but the MP3 files are actually transferred through the Internet and not Napster's web site. And if Napster met the service provider requirement of DCMA, it did not provide written notice that infringers would be terminated or take measures to prevent repeated infringement. The district court issued a preliminary injunction, finding that Napster users directly infringed the A & M copyrights and that downloading MP3 files to see whether one would like to purchase them does not constitute a "fair use." Napster appealed.)

With regard to Napster's defense of fair use, the court affirmed the district court's findings that users downloading MP3 files to "sample" the music and space-shifting do not constitute a fair use. In reviewing the plaintiff's claim for contributory infringement, the court found that Napster not only knew that its users committing copyright infringement, but also materially assisted them in such infringement because the users could not share the files without the Napster web site and software. Regarding the issue of vicarious liability, the court determined that Napster received financial benefits from an ever-increasing user base that was dependent on the availability of infringing material. Also, since Napster acted in a supervisory capacity by terminating users when it received complaints, the court determined that Napster met the requirements of vicarious liability. Finally, the court affirmed the district court's rejection of Napster's affirmative defenses under the Audio Home Recording Act and the Digital Millennium Copyright Act. Therefore, while the court affirmed the preliminary injunction, it slightly modified its scope.

3. New enforcement issues in copyright law

The Motorola, MP3.com, and Napster cases all have had enforcement of copyright protection as an underlying issue.

By its very nature, the Internet allows just about anyone to access copyrighted material, and then provides them with the opportunity to copy, manipulate, and distribute the underlying copyrighted material freely to the public. In enforcing the rights of the copyright holders, someone needs to be held accountable.

However, since most of the infringers are the invisible man (e.g., everyday individuals), there is little money or success in pursuing him. Therefore, the fear exists that in most cases, the copyright owners will go after the "deep pocket" service provider, and charge them with either direct, contributory, or vicarious copyright infringement since they provide the medium for sharing, copying, and posting of the unauthorized copyrighted material. However, if these providers are found liable for the copyright infringement of third parties, many worry that the Internet and ongoing technology would be stunted.

B. Digital Millennium Copyright Act of 1998

Congress in the Digital Millennium Copyright Act ("DCMA") addressed the tension between copyright protection and digital technology of 1998 (Public Law 105-304).

DCMA exchanges service provider liability protections for safeguards and other actions to protect copyrighted material and prevent ongoing infringement.

DCMA is divided into 5 Titles:

Title I. WIPO Treaties Implementation
Title II. Online Copyright Infringement Liability Limitation Act
Title III. Computer Maintenance or Repair Copyright Exemption
Title IV. Miscellaneous Provisions
Title V. Protection of Certain Original Designs

1. Title I. WIPO Treaties Implementation

Title I of DCMA is referred to as the "WIPO Copyright and Performances and Phonograms Treaties Implementation Act of 1998." This title implements the WIPO treaties by requiring the U.S. copyright law to:

(a) Extend US copyright law protections to works of individuals from other member nations that have not fallen into the public domain in the country of origin (foreign works are exempted from the formalities requirements of § 411(a).

(b) Adds a new sui generis chapter 12 to Title 17, which requires member countries to provide effective protection against circumvention of copyright protection systems and maintaining the integrity of copyright management information.

(i) Section 1201, however, still recognizes the affirmative defense of fair use and one may be justified in circumventing copy protection schemes in order to make fair use copies of a work.

(ii) Section 1201(d)-(j) provides exemptions to the circumventing provisions for the following:
§ 1201(d) - Nonprofit libraries, archives and educational institutions
§ 1202(e) - Law enforcement, intelligence, and other government activities
§ 1202(f) - Reverse engineering
§ 1202(g) - Encryption research
§ 1202(h) - Exceptions regarding minors
§ 1202(i) - Protection of personally identifying information (privacy)
§ 1202(j) - Security testing

(iii) Section 1202 prohibits anyone from knowingly providing or distributing false Copyright Management Information
(iv) Sections 1203 and 1204 outline the civil and criminal penalties for violating Sections 1201 or 1202.

2. Title II. Online Copyright Infringement Liability Limitation Act

Title II creates a new § 512 to the Copyright Act, which limits liability for service providers for:

(a) Transitory digital network communications (§512(a))
(b) System caching (§512(b))
(c) Information residing on systems or networks at direction of users (§512(c))
(d) Information Location Tools (§512(d))
(e) Nonprofit educational institutions (§512(e))

To qualify for any of these exemptions, under §512(i), the service provider must:

(1) Adopt and reasonably implement a policy of terminating the accounts of repeat infringers; and
(2) Accommodate and not obstruct "standard technical measures."

The eligibility requirements are:

(1) The provider cannot have actual knowledge of the infringement and must respond quickly to block or remove any infringing material as soon as the provider receives knowledge or notice;
(2) The provider cannot receive a financial benefit from the infringement; and
(3) The provider must quickly remove or block access to the infringing work as soon as the provider receives notice of the claim of copyright infringement from its designated agent, which must be filed with the Copyright Office.

3. Title III. Computer Maintenance or Repair Copyright Exemption

Title III of DCMA is referred to as the "Computer Maintenance Competition Assurance Act." It amends 17

U.S.C. § 117 to allow the owners of computer program to make copies of a computer program for the purpose only of maintaining or repairing that a computer, provided the new copy is destroyed immediately after the maintenance or repair is completed.

4. Title IV. Miscellaneous Provisions

Below are a few of the topics covered by Title IV of DCMA:

Ephemeral Recordings

Section 402 of DCMA amends 17 U.S.C. § 112 to give a transmitting organization that is a broadcast radio or television station licensed by the FCC to make ephemeral recordings in order to digitally transmit a sound recording on a nonsubscription basis. Additionally, § 405 discusses the scope of exclusive rights in sound and ephemeral recordings.

Exemption for Libraries and Archives

Section 404 of DCMA amends 17 U.S.C. § 107 to exempt libraries and archives from placing copyright notices on copies the library or archive makes unless the original work bears a copyright notice. Also, libraries and archives are permitted to make up to 3 copies (instead of 1) of either digital or analog phonorecords, provided those copies are not distributed in that format or made available to the public outside the library or archive.

5. Title V. Protection of Certain Original Designs

Title V of DCMA is referred to as the "Vessel Hull Design Project Act," and is added to the Copyright Act as new chapter 13. It applies to any boat hull that is not longer than 200 feet that possesses "an original design of a useful article." The application of the boat hull design must be filed within 2 years of making the design public and the term of the copyright will be 10 years from the earlier of the date of registration or publication.

This provision represents the first statute that provides copyright protection for a design of a useful article with no mention of conceptual separability.

X. APPLICATION FORMS

A. Original Registrations:

1. Form Group/Daily Newspapers: Registers complete month's issues of daily newspapers.
2. Form PA: Registers published and unpublished performing arts works.
3. Short Form/SE and Form SE/GROUP: Specialized SE forms
4. Form SE: Registers serial works that are issued in successive parts bearing numerical identification (volume 1, issue 1) and are meant to be continuous.
5. Form SR: Registers sound recording
6. Form TX: Registers published and unpublished non dramatic literary works.
7. Form VA: Registers published and unpublished visual arts.

B. Renewal Registrations

Form RE: Applies to claims to renewals under the laws effective through December 31, 1977 (1909 Copyright Act)

C. Corrections/Amplifications

Form CA.

D. Group of Contributions to Periodicals

1. Form GR/CP; and either
2: Form PA, TX, or VA.

XI. REGISTERING A COPYRIGHT

A. General

1. Most copyright registrations are easy and straightforward;
2. Proper computer software registration is much more difficult and an experienced attorney should always be consulted;
3. Prepare copyright application; and
4. Deposit the requisite number of copies with the U.S. Copyright Office.

- *Exception*: Software, because of trade secrets, the applicant may be allowed to deposit something less than a copy.

B. Fees (effective July 1, 1999)

1. Currently the fee for a basic registration is $30 per each application;
2. One can register a group of related claims (where appropriate) according to the following schedule:
   Serials (Form SE/Group) is $10/serial issue ($30 minimum)
   Daily newspapers and newsletters (Form G/DN) is $55
   Restored works (Form GATT/Grp) is $10/restored work ($30 minimum);
3. To correct or amplify a completed registration (Supplementary registration), there is a $65 fee; and
4. The U.S. Copyright Office can act on an expedited basis and the current fee is $500 per each application. (This is typically used if the work is going to be, or is currently involved in litigation.) This amount is in addition to the standard filing fee.*
   ($25 effective July 1, 1999).

C. Procedure for Registering

1. Completed application form;
2. Submit nonrefundable filing fee for each application; and
3. A nonreturnable copy (or copies) of work.

Send together to:
Register of Copyrights,
Copyright Office, Library of Congress,
Washington, D.C. 20559

***Expedited applications** should be mailed to:
Special Handling
Library of Congress
Dept. 100
Washington, D.C. 20540

D. Procedure for Renewal

1. Property completed RE., Application; and
2. Nonrefundable $45 fee for each work effective July 1, 1999. The fee for an addendum to a renewal form is $15.

E. Incomplete Submissions

If the three elements under Procedure for Registering are not received together, the application will not be processed. Ordinarily, any incomplete submission is returned with notice of why it was not processed.

F. Effective Date of Registration

The effective date of registration is when the U.S. Copyright Office receives all of the required elements. It takes approximately 16 weeks to receive a certificate of registration if application is submitted for regular processing, or only 10 days if applicant submits application for special handling (expedited service).

Statutory Reference to Selected Copyright Topics

Topic	1976 Act	1909 Act
Fixation	§§101 ("copies," "devices, machine or process," "fixed," "phonorecords"), 102(a).	§ 4.
Originality	§§ 101 ("created"), 102(a) and (b).	§ 4.
Works of Authorship	§§ 101 ("audiovisual works," "computer program," "including" and "such as," "literary works," "motion pictures," "pictorial, graphic, and sculptural works," "sound recordings," "useful articles"), 102.	§§ 3-6.
Architectural Works	§§ 101 ("architectural works," "Berne Convention work"), 102(a)(8), 120, 301(b)(4).	Not included
Derivative Works and Compilations	§§ 101 ("collective work," "compilation," "derivative work"), 103.	§ 7
Exclusive Rights	§ 106	§ 1
Visual Artists Rights Act of 1990	§§ 101 ("work of visual art"), 106A, 113(d), 301(f)	Not included
Ownership	§§ 101 ("copyright owner," "joint work," "work made for hire"), 201(a)-(c)	§ 26
Transfer of Rights	§§ 101 ("transfer of copyright ownership"), 201(d)-(e), 202, 204-05	§§ 27-32
Duration and Renewal	§§ 101 ("anonymous work," "children," "joint work," "pseudonymous work," "widow" and "widower," "work made for hire"), 302, 303, 304(a) and (b), 305; Transitional and Supplementary Provisions §§ 102-03, 107	§§ 22-25
Termination	§§ 203, ß 304(c)	Not included
Publication	§§ 101 ("Berne Convention work," "publication"), 304, 401-02, 405-07; Transitional and Supplementary Provisions § 103	§§ 2, 7, 10, 12-13, 22-23, 26
Notice	§§ 101 ("best edition," "publicly"), 401-06; Transitional and Supplementary Provisions § 108	§§ 8, 10, 19-21
Infringement	§§ 501, 511	§ 115

SUMMARY FOR SELECTED SECTIONS OF THE COPYRIGHT ACT OF 1976

17 U.S.C.

The following terms are defined in (§ 101):

"Anonymous Work"
"Architectural Work"
"Audiovisual Work"
"Berne Convention"
"Berne Convention Work"
"Best Edition"
"Children"
"Collective Work"
"Compilation"
"Computer Program"
"Copies"
"Copyright Origin"
"Copyright Owner
"Country of Ownership"
"Created"
"Derivative Work"
"Device," "Machine,"
"Digital Transmission"
"Display"
"Financial Gain"
"Fixed"
"Government"
"Including" and "Such As"
"Joint Work"
"Literary Works"
"Motion Pictures"
"Perform"
"Phonorecords"
"Pseudonymous Work"
"Publication"
"Publicity"
"Registration"
"Sound Recordings"
"State"
"Transfer of Copyright"
"Transmission Program"
"Transmit"
"United States"
"Process"
"Useful Article"
"Widow" or "Widower"
"Work of Visual Art"
"Work of the United States"
"Work Made For Hire"

CONTINUATION OF SUMMARY FOR SELECTED SECTIONS OF THE COPYRIGHT ACT OF 1976

I. General subject Matter of Copyright (§ 102)

A. Material Object Defined
   1. Copies - all material objects which are not phonorecords.
   2. Phonorecords - sound objects

B. Two Criteria
   1. Originality
      a. Purposefully undefined;
      b. No requirement of novelty, ingenuity, or [a] esthetic merit;
      c. Others may use ideas or information revealed by the author.
   2. Fixation in a Tangible Form
      a. Only writings may receive federal copyright protection.
      b. Any physical rendering of the fruits of the writing.
      c. Fixed Medium of Expression Necessary
         (1) Copy or phonorecord;
         (2) Sufficiently permanent or stable;
             * Now known or later developed.
         (3) Work is perceived, reproduced or otherwise communicated for longer than a temporary time.
             (i) May be aided by machine
             (ii) May be aided by other device.
                  * Unfixed works do not receive federal protection, however, they do receive protection under State common law or statute.

C. Illustrative Categories
   1. Musical works
   2. Dramatic works
   3. Pantomimes and choreographic works
   4. Literary works
   5. Pictorial, graphic, and sculptural works
      a. No need for artistic taste or [a] esthetic value

b. All original works intended to be useful articles regardless _of mass production, commercial exploration or potential patent protection (*Mazur v. Stein*).
   Useful article is one where the article has a intrinsic utilitarian function that does more than portray the article's information.
c. Form but not mechanical aspects of work protected.
d. Includes diagrams, models and technical drawing (architectural designs).

6. Motion pictures and audiovisual works
   a. A series of image;
   b. The capability of showing images in certain successive order;
   c. An impression of motion when the images are shown;
   d. Does not include the following:
      (i) Unauthorized fixation of live performances or telecasts;
      (ii) Live telecasts that are not fixed simultaneously with their transmission;
      (iii) Filmstrips and slide sets which, although consisting of a series of images intended to be shown in succession, are not capable of conveying and impression of motion.
7. Sound recording
   a. Original works that are musical, spoken or other sounds that have been fixed in a tangible form.
   b. Motion picture soundtracks are under the motion picture section.

D. Is a Writing a Work of Authorship?
   1. Determine if the legislative history has expressly excluded it. Such as industrial or typeface design.
   2. Absent exclusion determine whether the writing has been historically excluded. Such as literary characters and title.

II. Compilations and Derivative Works (§ 102)

A. Compilations - process of selecting, bringing together, organizing and arranging previously existing material of all kinds, regardless whether the individual items are subject to copyright.

B. Derivative - process of recasting, transforming, or adapting one or more previous works. However, the preexisting work must be within § 102 General Subject Matter regardless whether it was actually copyrighted.

III. Exclusive Rights in Copyrighted Works (§ 106)

A. Five exclusive fundamental rights to copyright owners:
   1. Reproduction;
   2. Adaptation;
   3. Publication;
   4. Performance;
   5. Display.

B. Subject to §§ 107-20

IV. Ownership of Copyright (§ 201)

A. Initial Owner
   1. Author owns copyright
   2. Joint-authors
      a. Joint
         (i) Collaboration;
         (ii) Each prepared their contribution with knowledge and intention that it be merged with the other;
         (iii) To make an inseparable work.

B. Works Made for Hire
   1. Employer is the author unless agreement.
   2. Agreement must be in writing and signed by the parties.

C. Contributions to Collective Works
   1. Collective work is a type of compilation.
   2. Each collective work must be a separate and independent work.
   3. Author's copyright in the individual piece is preserved, in other words, there is no transfer of rights.

D. Transfer
   1. Copyright may be transferred by any means.
   2. Copyright is considered personal property.
   3. Transfer must be voluntary for the rights to transfer

V. Distinction Between Ownership of Copyright and Material Object (§ 202)

VI. Termination of Transfers and Licenses (§ 203)

A. Scope
   1. Advance notice within specified time limits.
   2. Includes any transfer of copyright ownership and any non-exclusive license.

B. Who May Terminate a Grant
   1. Two issues of dispute.
      a. The specific class of beneficiaries in the case of joint works.
      b. Whether anything less that unanimous consent can effectively terminate the grant.
   2. Majority of joint authors who signed the grant may terminate.
   3. Three situations in which the shares of joint authors (or their survivors) must divided under the statute:
      a. The right to effect a termination;
      b. The ownership of the terminated rights;
      c. The right to make further grants of reverted rights.
   4. Survivors who receive rights take them under a per stirpes share.

C. When Can a Grant be Terminated
   1. Five years following the expiration of a period of 35 years from the execution of the grant.

   Exception: If the grant includes right of publication the period is 35 years from the date of publication of work under grant or at the end of 40 years from date of execution of the grant, whichever term ends first.

2. Advance notice must be provided before the 5 year window.

D. Effect of Termination
1. Reverts ownership who owns termination interest on date termination was served regardless whether they signed the notice or not.
2. If not effectively terminated within the 5 year window all rights will continue unchanged.

VII. Execution and Recordation of Transfers (§ 204, § 205)

A. Valid transfer
1. Need writing
    a. Instrument of conveyance; or
    b. A note or memorandum of the transfer.
2. Signed by copyright owner or duly authorized agent.

B. Constructive notice of contents of writing:
1. The document or attached material specifically identifies the work so that a reasonable search of title or registration number would reveal it; and
2. Registration has been made for the work.

C. Non-exclusive license in writing and signed are valid against any later transfer regardless or recording.

VIII. Federal Preemption of Rights Equivalent to Copyright (§ 302)

A. Protected upon creation or when it is "fixed in a copy or phonorecord for the first time".

B. Arguments for the federal system:
1. Promotes national uniformity;
2. Helps give a clear interpretation of publication;
3. § 301 will implant the limited times provisions of the Constitution;
4. Need for effective international copyright relations.

IX. Duration of Copyright in Works Created After Effective Date (§ 302)

A. General
   1. Life of author and last 70 years after author's death.
   2. 1909 Act
      a. Begins date of publication.
      b. Continues 28 years from that date.
      c. May be renewed for a second 28 years (total of 56 years).
      d. Arguments for changing time based on author's life;
         (i) The present 56 year term is not long enough to insure author hand his dependents the fair economic benefits from his work.
         (ii) The tremendous growth in communications media as substantially lengthened the commercial life of a great many works.
         (iii) Although limitations on the term of copyright are obviously necessary, too short a term harms the author without giving any substantial benefit to the public.
         (iv) A system based on the life of an author would go a long way toward clearing up the confusion and uncertainty involved in the vague concept of "publication," and would provide a much simpler, clearer method for computing the term.
         (v) One of the worst features of the present copyright law is the provision for renewal of copyright. Under a life-plus 70 system the renewal device would be inappropriate and unnecessary.
         (vi) Under the preemption provisions of § 301 and the single federal system they would establish that authors will be giving up perpetual, unlimited exclusive common law rights in their unpublished works, including works that have been widely disseminated by means other than publication.
         (vii)A very large majority of countries have adapted a copyright term of the life of the

author plus years after the author's death. Since American authors are frequently protected longer in foreign countries than in the United States, the disparity in the duration of copyright has provoked considerable resentment and some proposals for retaliatory legislation. A change in the basis of our copyright term would place the United States in the forefront of the international copyright community.

B. Under § 302, a work created after the death of the revise statute is protected for the life of the author plus 70 years.

C. Joint works are measured by the longest surviving author.

D. Anonymous Works, Pseudonymous and Works for Hire
   1. Protected for 95 years from publication or 120 years from creation, whichever is longer.
   2. Can be converted to life of author plus 70 years if the author is "revealed" in special records maintained by the Copyright Office.

E. Records and Presumption as to Author's Death
   1. § 302(d) and (e) furnish an answer to practical problems of how to discover the death dates of obscure or unknown authors.

X. Preexisting Works Under Common Law Protection (§ 303)

A. Copyrights will not expire before December 31, 2002 and attempts to encourage publication by providing 45 years more protection if the work were published before the end of 2002,
B. Protected as long as the work is not public domain in the United States.

XI. Duration of Subsisting copyrights (§ 304)

A. Increases present 56 years to 95 years in the case of copyrights subsisting in both their first and renewal term.

B. In the case of a renewal after the effective date but original copyright was prior maybe terminated under certain conditions and limitations.
The 5 year window during which termination could be made effective would start 56 years after copyright was originally secured.

C. Copyrights in their First Term
   1. Preserves the renewal provision for all works in their first 28 year term.
   2. Renewal registration needed during the 28th year of copyright but length of renewal will be increased from 28 to 67 years.

D. Copyrights in their Renewal Term
   1. Copyrights in their 2nd term at any time during December 31, 1976 and December 31, 1977 (inclusively) would be extended to a total of 95 years.
   2. Adds another 39 years to any renewed copyright whose 2nd term stated during the 28 years immediately preceding January 1, 1978 (effective date).
   3. If renewal is to take place within the prior year of the_ effective date, the copyright is treated as in the second term and is automatically extended for 95 years.

XII. Year End Expirations of Terms (§ 305)

A. Copyright protection extend till December 31 of the year in which the term would have expired.
Applies only to terms of copyright provided by §§ 302-04.

B. Renewal must be made within 1 year prior to the terminating December 31 date.

XIII. Notice on Visually-Perceptible Copies (§ 401)

A. Copyright Notice Functions:
   1. It has the effect of placing in the public domain a substantial body of published material that no one is interested in copyrighting;
   2. It informs the public as to whether a particular work is copyrighted;

3. It identifies the copyright owner; and
4. It shows the date of publication.

B. Notice on visually perceptible copies:
1. "Copyright"; or
2. "Copr."; or
3. "©."

C. No need to list date of publication of preexisting compilation works.

D. Recognizable abbreviation of copyright owners are acceptable.

E. Fixed in a location and manner to give reasonable notice of claim to copyright.

XIV. Notice of Phonorecords of Sound Recordings (§ 402)

A. General
1. Use the Symbol "P";
2. Name of the sound recording; and
3. Name of the copyright owner or an admissible variant.

B. Three reasons for using "P" instead of the "©":
1. Avoid confusion between copyright in the sound recording an in the musical or literary work embodied in it;
2. Distinguishes between copyright claims in the sound recording and in the printed test or art work appearing on the record label, album cover, etc.; and
3. Symbol "P_" has been adopted as the international symbol for the protection of sound recordings.

XV. Notice for Publications Incorporating United States Works (§403)

A. Requires that when the copies or phonorecords consist "predominantly of 1 or more works of the United States Government," the copyright notice (if any) identify those parts of the work in which the copyright is claimed.

XVI. Notice for Contributions to Collective Works (§ 404)

A. Basic Approach:
   1. To permit but not require a separate contribution to bear its own notice;
   2. To make a single notice, covering the collective work as a whole, sufficient to satisfy the notice requirement for the separate contributions it contains, even if they have been previously published or their ownership is different; and
   3. To protect the interests of an innocent infringer of copyright in a contribution that does not bear its own notice, who has dealt in good faith with the person named in the notice covering the collective work as a whole.

B. Separate contribution published with no notice of owner is treated as if it was published with the wrong name in the notice.

XVII. Omission of Copyright Notice (§ 405)

A. Protected 5 years even if omission was partial or total, unintentional or deliberate.

B. Omission of notice does not invalidate the copyright if either:
   1. If "no more than a relatively small number of copies or phonorecords have been publicly distributed without notice; or
   2. If registration for the work has already been made, or is made within 5 years after the publication without notice, and a reasonable effort is made to add notice to copies or phonorecords publicly distributed in the United States after the omission is discovered (unlike the 1909 Act).

C. Current notice requirements
   1. Unchanged for works first published before the effective date of the Act.

2. Will be public domain if published without notice, and registration is not made before or within 5 years of publication.

XVIII. Prerequisite for Statutory Damages and Attorney's fees (§412)

Election of Statutory Damages and Attorney's fees not available if:

1. The copyright infringement of an unpublished work began before the effective date of its registration; or

2. The copyright infringement began after first publication of the work and before the effective date of its registration, unless the registration is made within 3 months of the first publication.

XIX. Infringement of copyright (§ 501)

A. Defined as someone "who violates any of the exclusive rights of the copyright owner as provided by §§ 106-20" of the bill, or who imports copies or phonorecords in violation of § 602.

B. Owner may sue for infringement while protecting rights of other possible owners whose rights might be protected.
   1. Allows original owner of collective or derivative works to be joined in the suit for infringement.
   2. Allows joinder of beneficial owner who is an author who had parted with legal title to the copyright in exchange for percentage of royalties based upon sales or license fees.

C. Related or Vicarious Infringer
   1. Actively operate or supervise the operation of the place wherein the performances occur; or
   2. Control the content of the infringing program, and expect commercial gain from the operation and either
      a. Direct; or
      b. Indirect benefit from the infringing performance

XX. Remedies for Infringement: (§ 502)

Court may grant temporary and permanent injunctions for copyright infringement.

XXI. Remedies for Infringement: Costs and Attorney's Fees (§ 505)

An infringer of copyright is liable for either-

1. the copyright owner's actual damages and any additional profits of the infringer; or
2. Statutory damages.

XXII. Remedies for infringement: Costs and attorney's fees (§ 505)

Courts have discretion to award the prevailing party of an action recovery of its full costs and/or attorney's fees.

TABLE OF CASES

INDEX

A

B

C

H

I

J

L

M

N

O

P

R

S

T

U

V

W

Y